ANIMALS

THE STRANGE AND EXCITING STORIES OF THEIR LIVES

by
Bertel Bruun, M.D.
Illustrated by
Dorothea and Sy Barlowe

Collins Glasgow and London

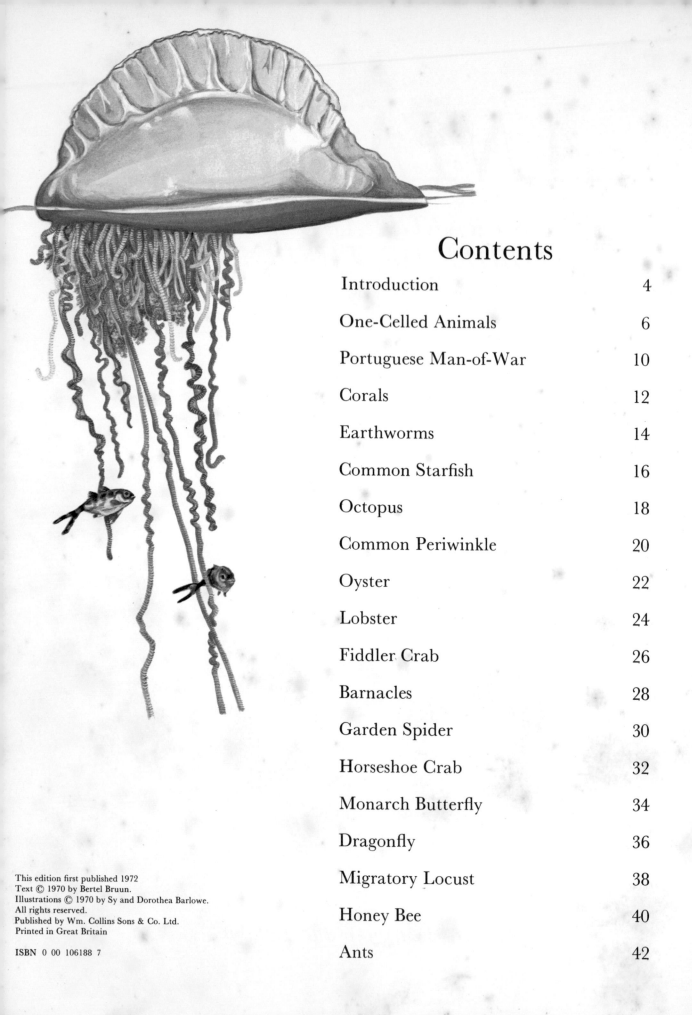

Contents

This edition first published 1972
Text © 1970 by Bertel Bruun.
Illustrations © 1970 by Sy and Dorothea Barlowe.
All rights reserved.
Published by Wm. Collins Sons & Co. Ltd.
Printed in Great Britain

ISBN 0 00 106188 7

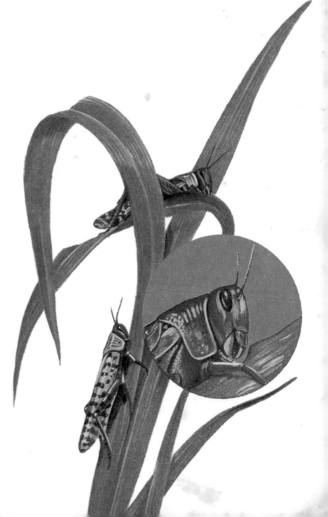

Introduction

Everyone can tell the difference between a dog and a bush. A dog, and most other animals, can move about; a plant hardly moves at all. Some animals eat plants, some prey upon and eat other animals; some animals do both. A plant makes its own food: with the help of a green substance called chlorophyll, it can use the light from the sun to make food out of the carbon dioxide from the air and the water soaked up from the ground.

Both plants and animals probably developed from the same kind of plant-animal. Some such microscopic one-celled organisms called flagellates have both the chlorophyll with which they can produce food and the ability to eat other plants and move about. They are really neither plants nor animals, but something in between.

There are other kinds of life that are neither animals nor plants. The simplest ones are so small that they cannot be seen under any ordinary microscope. They are called viruses. Small as they are, they live and multiply, although they have to be inside the cells of other living organisms to multiply. Some viruses cause diseases like chicken pox and measles.

A little larger than the viruses are the bacteria. They can be seen in the microscope. Bacteria can produce energy from different sources, but they do not have chlorophyll like plants. Some bacteria cause diseases like scarlet fever and pneumonia.

All animals and plants are made up of cells. Most plant cells have thick walls of a strong material called cellulose. Most animal cells have only a thin membrane.

The Animal Cell

All animals are built up of cells. Some animals, like the amoeba, consist of just one cell. Other animals are made up of millions of cells. Each cell can perform all the different life processes. It can use oxygen ("breathe"), grow, and even divide into two or more complete cells.

Most cells are so small that they can be seen only with a microscope. When seen through a microscope, the cell can be studied more closely. It consists of a cytoplasm ("cell-form") surrounded by a thin membrane. Inside the cytoplasm a round body is seen, the nucleus. Inside the nucleus is the chromatin. Chromatin carries a kind of code that plans the development of the cell. Also in the cytoplasm are small vacuoles that contain food and waste material. Other parts of the cytoplasm contain substances that are necessary for the digestion of food and the building up of the material needed for the growth of the cell. All in all, though, three-quarters of the cell consists of water.

Most animals are made up of a lot of different kinds of cells. Each kind of cell has its own function. Muscle cells can contract; gland cells can form and secrete special chemicals; blood cells can take up and release oxygen; bone cells can build up strong bone; covering cells form the protecting outer surface skin; hair cells form hair; fat cells store fat; nerve cells conduct impulses from one part of the body to another; and so on and so on.

Animals can reproduce. This means they can have young that are similar to themselves. Some animals reproduce simply by dividing into two. This is called asexual reproduction because only one sex, not both male and female, is involved. However, most animals, reproduce sexually. This means that both the female and the male are necessary for reproduction. The female has special glands that produce egg cells. The male has special glands that produce sperm. The egg cell unites with a sperm cell to form one new cell, a fertilized egg. The fertilized egg then starts growing, and it eventually grows to be an individual like its father or mother.

The Animal Kingdom

There are thousands and thousands of different kinds of animals. Scientists have divided all animals into groups. Within each group are the animals most closely related. These groups are then arranged in such a way as to start with the simplest kind of animals—the one-celled animals—and end up with the most complicated—mammals. In that way one can draw a family tree of all animals. A main group of animals is called a phylum. Each phylum is divided into classes, each class into orders, and each order into families. For instance, the human being belongs to the phylum Chordata (animals with backbones), the class mammals, the order primates, and the family homo, of which we are the only species living today.

Life Processes

To stay alive and reproduce, every animal has to have certain life processes. First they have to be able to obtain food and use it. Most animals have a mouth through which the food enters the digestive tract, or gut. In the gut, food is broken down (digested) and absorbed by the blood, which then transports the food to all cells in the body. The waste from the food is eliminated either through an opening in the digestive tract, the anus, or through special organs, kidneys, that filter the waste and form urine. The food has to be burned for the animal to get energy from it. This takes place in the cell. Food inside the body is used up very slowly; but, as when a match burns, oxygen is needed for the process. Oxygen is a gas that is found in the air. It dissolves in water. Most animals have special organs for extracting oxygen from the air or water—fish have gills, and mammals have lungs. The oxygen is then carried to all the cells by the blood cells. When the food has been burned, carbon dioxide is formed. This is also a gas, and it is transported back to the lungs or gills by the blood cells. In the lungs or gills it is given into the air or the water.

Most animals can move. They can move away from enemies. They can move towards their food. Movement is a very complicated process that in most animals involves some nerve cells that observe the surroundings and other nerve cells that send messages out to the muscle cells, which move the animal. Many special organs have developed for animals to be able to observe their surroundings: eyes, ears, taste buds, and sensitive hair (such as a cat's whiskers) are just a few examples.

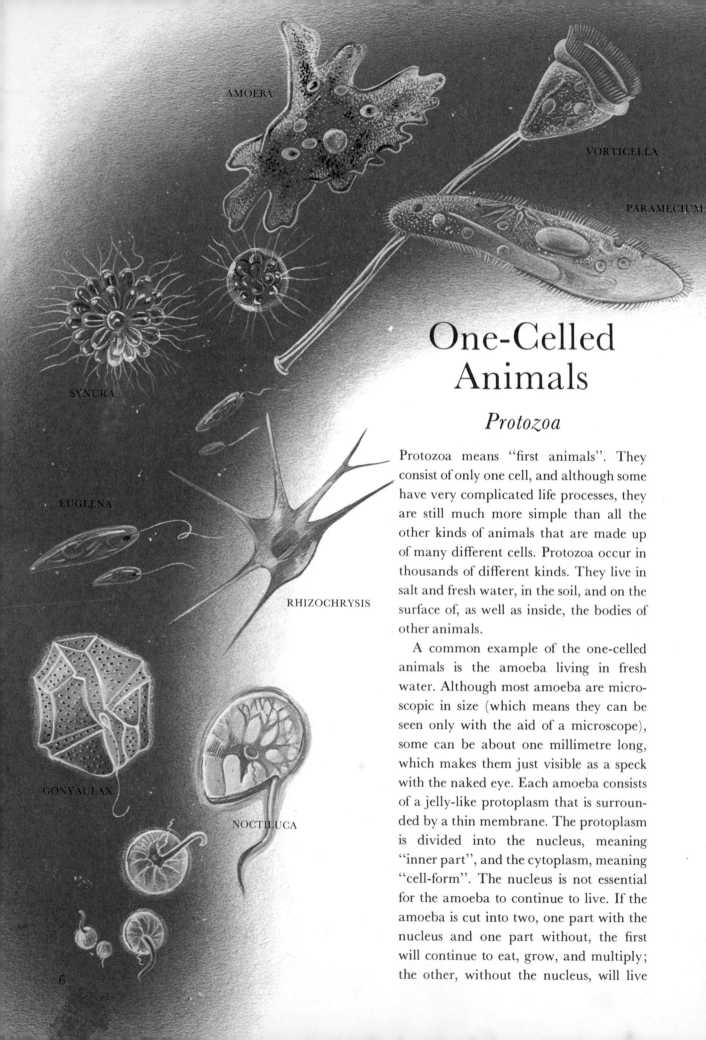

AMOEBA

VORTICELLA

PARAMECIUM

SYNURA

EUGLENA

RHIZOCHRYSIS

GONYAULAX

NOCTILUCA

One-Celled Animals

Protozoa

Protozoa means "first animals". They consist of only one cell, and although some have very complicated life processes, they are still much more simple than all the other kinds of animals that are made up of many different cells. Protozoa occur in thousands of different kinds. They live in salt and fresh water, in the soil, and on the surface of, as well as inside, the bodies of other animals.

A common example of the one-celled animals is the amoeba living in fresh water. Although most amoeba are microscopic in size (which means they can be seen only with the aid of a microscope), some can be about one millimetre long, which makes them just visible as a speck with the naked eye. Each amoeba consists of a jelly-like protoplasm that is surrounded by a thin membrane. The protoplasm is divided into the nucleus, meaning "inner part", and the cytoplasm, meaning "cell-form". The nucleus is not essential for the amoeba to continue to live. If the amoeba is cut into two, one part with the nucleus and one part without, the first will continue to eat, grow, and multiply; the other, without the nucleus, will live

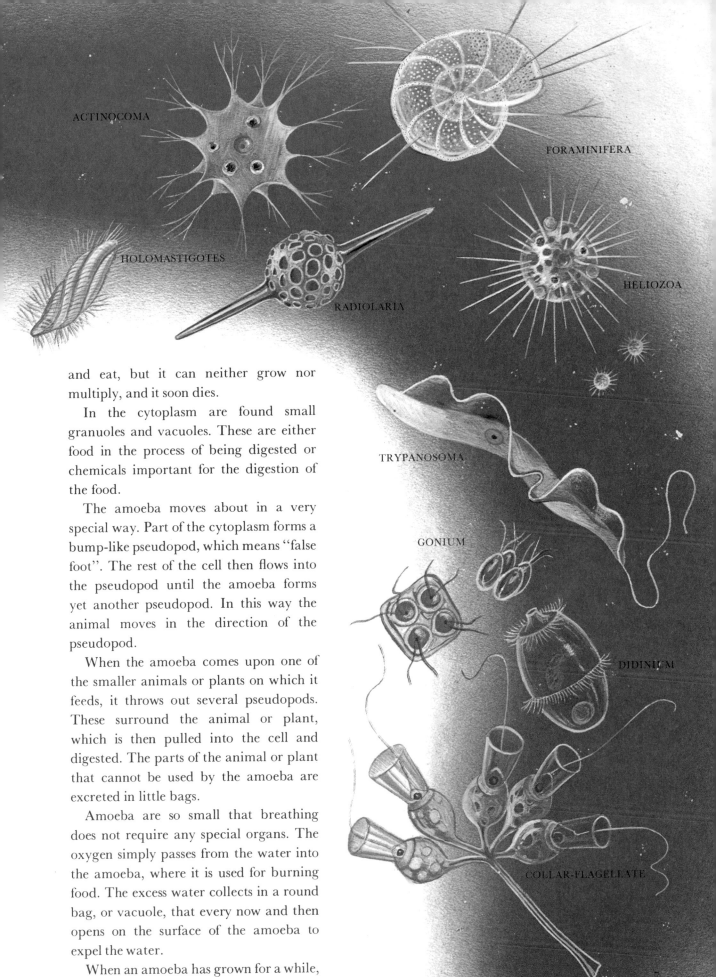

ACTINOCOMA

FORAMINIFERA

HOLOMASTIGOTES

RADIOLARIA

HELIOZOA

TRYPANOSOMA

GONIUM

DIDINIUM

COLLAR-FLAGELLATE

and eat, but it can neither grow nor multiply, and it soon dies.

In the cytoplasm are found small granuoles and vacuoles. These are either food in the process of being digested or chemicals important for the digestion of the food.

The amoeba moves about in a very special way. Part of the cytoplasm forms a bump-like pseudopod, which means "false foot". The rest of the cell then flows into the pseudopod until the amoeba forms yet another pseudopod. In this way the animal moves in the direction of the pseudopod.

When the amoeba comes upon one of the smaller animals or plants on which it feeds, it throws out several pseudopods. These surround the animal or plant, which is then pulled into the cell and digested. The parts of the animal or plant that cannot be used by the amoeba are excreted in little bags.

Amoeba are so small that breathing does not require any special organs. The oxygen simply passes from the water into the amoeba, where it is used for burning food. The excess water collects in a round bag, or vacuole, that every now and then opens on the surface of the amoeba to expel the water.

When an amoeba has grown for a while,

7

it divides into two parts. First the nucleus breaks up and is divided into two equal parts. Then the cytoplasm divides into two, each part with its own nucleus. Each new amoeba then starts eating and growing. This kind of reproduction is called asexual because there is only one cell involved from the beginning.

If the water in which the amoeba lives dries up, the amoeba can secrete a fluid that forms a hard shell as it dries. Inside this shell, or cyst, as it is also called, the amoeba can stay alive for a long time. If the water returns, the amoeba comes out of its cyst and starts moving about as before.

Protozoa can have many different forms which vary from the rounded shape of the amoeba to the vorticella. The vorticella has a stalk with which it is attached to a piece of sand or stone. This stalk can

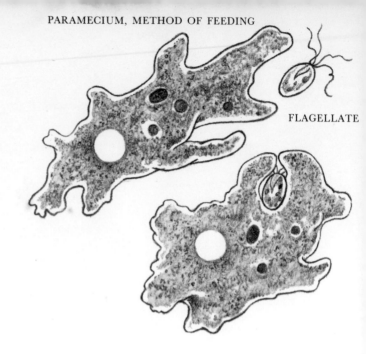

FLAGELLATE

contract and make the animal shorter. At the tip of the stalk is the main part of the animal. It is funnel-shaped, with cilia (small hairs) at the edge, which beat the water in such a way that when bacteria are nearby, the bacteria are moved closer to the vorticella and eaten.

One of the most complicated groups of protozoa is the paramecia. Paramecia live in fresh water where they eat bacteria. As opposed to the amoeba, which changes shape all the time, the paramecium has a constant shape. It is elongated almost in the form of a shoe. Along the sides there are more than two thousand tiny hairs, or cilia. By moving these back and forth the paramecium can swim very fast through the water. On one side there is a groove in

CILIA BEAT IN WAVES

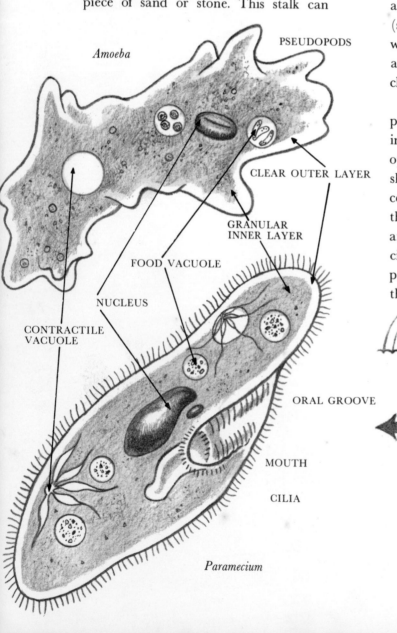

Amoeba

PSEUDOPODS

CLEAR OUTER LAYER

GRANULAR INNER LAYER

FOOD VACUOLE

NUCLEUS

CONTRACTILE VACUOLE

ORAL GROOVE

MOUTH

CILIA

Paramecium

The paramecium moves through the water in a spiral manner because the cilia in the oral groove are large and beat more vigorously

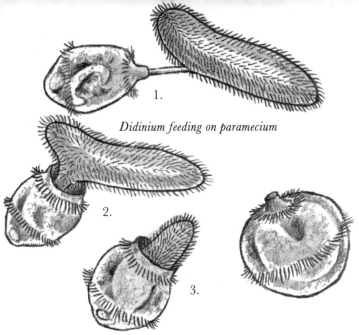

Didinium feeding on paramecium

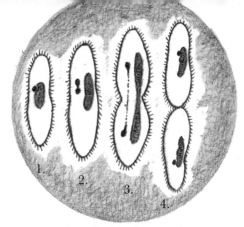

Reproduction of paramecium

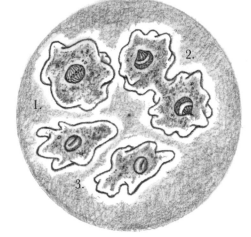

Reproduction of amoeba

the covering. This is where the bacteria are caught and eaten. When paramecia reproduce, they do so in the same way as the amoeba. One paramecium may divide several times a day, so in the course of two days it can become sixty-four paramecia. The paramecia also sometimes combine. Part of the nucleus of each wanders over into the other. They then separate and start dividing into several new paramecia. This is almost the same as what happens when a sperm fertilizes an egg. This is called sexual reproduction because parts of two cells are necessary.

Some protozoa are parasitic. A parasite is an animal or plant that lives by taking its food from another animal or plant. Some parasites cause disease. One such parasitic protozoa causing disease in man is the *plasmodium malariae*, which causes malaria. The parasite, which at this time is called a sporocyte, is injected into man when a mosquito bites him. The parasites enter the red blood corpuscles. Here they divide many times. When the red blood corpuscle is filled with parasites, it breaks, and each parasite then enters another red blood corpuscle. This can go on for a long time.

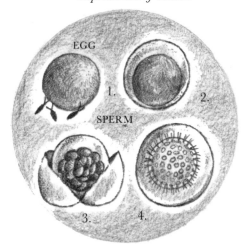

Sexual reproduction of volvox

Movement of amoeba by means of pseudopods

Reproduction of stalked-ciliate vorticella

Portuguese Man-of-War

Physalia

The brightly coloured Portuguese man-of-war is not just one animal. It is a whole group of animals forming a colony. It is found floating in the warm oceans, often several colonies together.

On the top, sticking out of the water, is a "sail". The sail is really a float, or gas-filled bladder. The gas is formed by special cells in the lower part of the sail. The sail catches the wind and carries the Portuguese man-of-war far and wide, even across the Atlantic Ocean. The sail can be up to 30 centimetres (12 inches) long.

Underneath the sail is the rest of the colony of animals forming the Portuguese man-of-war. Each member of the colony has its own function, much like the different tissues in higher animals. There are gastrozooids, which act like a stomach and digest food. There are so-called dactylozooids, which are long threads, or tentacles, that hang underneath and can

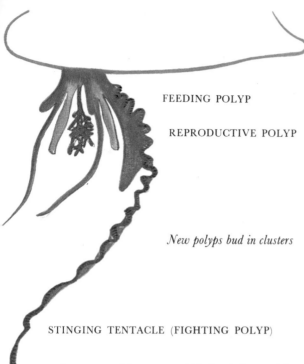

FEEDING POLYP

REPRODUCTIVE POLYP

New polyps bud in clusters

STINGING TENTACLE (FIGHTING POLYP)

be up to 12 metres (40 feet) long. They are of a brilliant blue colour. On them are stinging cells that are coiled up like springs. When something touches the tentacle, the spring is released, and the end shoots out into the water. The end has a sharp point which can go through the skin of fish and other animals. The sting is poisonous and can even kill small fish. Another animal that forms part of the Portuguese man-of-war is the gono-zooid. It acts as a sex gland and produces either eggs or sperm. The fertilized egg becomes the larva, which is very much like a grown-up Portuguese man-of-war except that it lacks the float. It looks like a jellyfish and is called a medusa.

Portuguese men-of-war live on fish that get too close to the tentacles. The stinging poison kills the fish. The tentacles seize

Food: fish

the fish and lift it up underneath the float to where the gastrozooids are. Each gastrozooid then covers a part of the fish and starts eating it. The nutrition from the food is carried round the colony through little canals that connect each individual in the colony.

There is one kind of fish that is not affected by the tentacles. It swims round them as if they were just ordinary sea-weed. Its latin name is *Nomeus gronovii*. It does not have a common name. This little fish attracts larger fish, which want to eat it but which are themselves eaten by the Portuguese man-of-war. The little fish then gets parts of the fish that the Portuguese man-of-war has caught. This kind of relationship between two animals, where both have an advantage in the relationship, is called a symbiosis.

Development of Portuguese man-of-war (numbers show successive stages of growth)

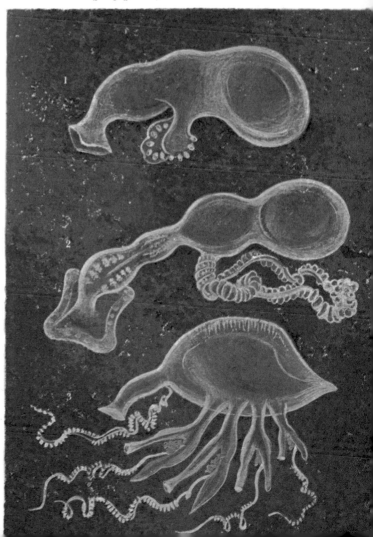

Corals

Corals belong to a large group of sea animals called *Coelenterata*. The word "coelenterate" means "hollow gut". The group owes its name to the fact that the main part of each animal is a large digestive tract.

There are many kinds of coelenterates. They are divided into three classes. One of these is called the hydrozoa. The Portuguese man-of-war belongs to this group. Hydra, from which these animals derive their name, was a fabled snake with many heads. When one head was cut off, a new one grew in its place. The Swedish naturalist, Linnaeus, gave the animals this name because cutting them into pieces did not kill them but only made each piece grow into a new animal. The second group is called scyphozoa, meaning "cup animals". Most jellyfish belong to this group.

The last class are the anthozoa, meaning "flower animals". The sea anemone is one of these. Sea anemones are found along coasts, attached to rocks on the bottom of the sea. A sea anemone consists of a body that is formed like a tube. One end is closed and forms the basal disc on which the animal sits. The other end is open. The opening is the mouth. The

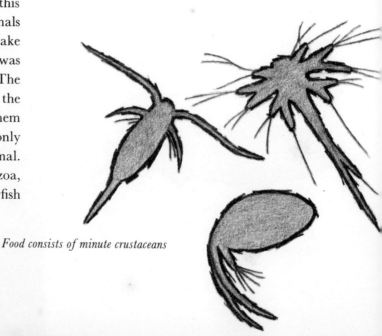

Food consists of minute crustaceans

mouth is surrounded by long threads or tentacles. These threads have stinging cells on them that can kill small fish and other animals. The sea anemone can close its mouth and pull in its tentacles so that it becomes almost flat.

The corals are very much like sea anemones, but their skin excretes lime. The lime forms a shell around them so that only the mouth with the tentacles sticks out. The basal disc is folded, so that if the animal dies only the shell and the starlike remnants of the basal disc are left behind.

Most corals live in colonies. The colony starts with a tiny little animal, the planula. The planula develops from an egg and a sperm inside the old coral. The planula swims about for a few days before it settles on the bottom of the sea and changes into a real coral animal. Soon it grows out another animal as a little bud. This it can do again and again, and so a colony of coral is formed. Each animal lives on small crustaceans (shrimplike animals) and other animals that it catches with its tentacles. Different corals form colonies that are different shapes. The brain coral has a folded surface. The star coral is covered with stars that are really the parts formed by the basal discs of the coral animals. The staghorn coral branches out like a tree. Most corals live in warm waters where millions and millions of corals form coral reefs. As one colony of corals dies, a new one settles on top of it, and a reef may grow from 5 centimetres (2 inches) to 180 centimetres (6 feet) per year. The Florida Keys were originally such a reef, as are many of the islands in the Pacific. The longest reef is the Great Barrier Reef of Australia, which is more than 900 kilometres (600 miles) from end to end.

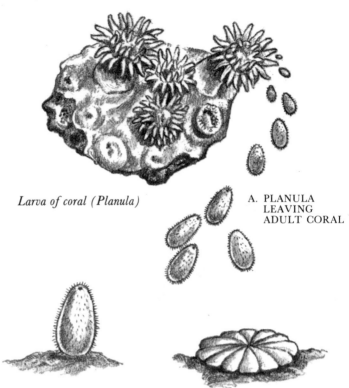

Larva of coral (Planula)

A. PLANULA LEAVING ADULT CORAL

B. PLANULA LANDS ON HARD SURFACE AND FLATTENS AS IT BEGINS TO GROW

C. YOUNG POLYP IN EARLY STAGE

D. CORAL POLYP IN MORE ADVANCED STAGE

Method of budding of a coral polyp

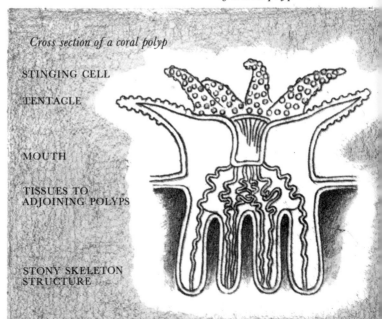

Cross section of a coral polyp

STINGING CELL

TENTACLE

MOUTH

TISSUES TO ADJOINING POLYPS

STONY SKELETON STRUCTURE

Earthworms

Lumbricidae

Earthworms spend most of their time underground. They dig their long tunnels several centimetres below the surface, and here they occur in countless numbers. They make their tunnels by swallowing the earth ahead of them, along with microscopic plants, rotting vegetation, insect eggs, and other kinds of food, which are absorbed into the intestine. The rest of the earth the worm has swallowed is deposited on the surface above as a small casting.

The body of an earthworm is long and streamlined. It consists of a number of segments, usually about seventy-five. The segments are the rings that can be seen on the worm. On each segment there are four pairs of bristles, or short hairs. The worm can protrude each of these hairs so that they can grip the side of the burrow. The worm also uses them for moving about. First it stretches the front part of its body forward. When the bristles there have a good hold, the worm pulls the

hind part up. In this way the worm can move at a speed of about $2\frac{1}{2}$ centimetres (one inch) per second.

At both ends a worm has light-sensitive cells that function as eyes. The cells can only react to changes in light, and the worm does not see formed things as we do. Worms can also detect vibrations in the earth. By poking a stick into the ground and moving it back and forth, one can get worms to leave their burrows.

The earthworm has no lungs or gills. It breathes through its skin, which is thin. The worm has to keep moist to be able to breathe in this way. When it rains, some worms come out of their burrows and onto the surface. This is because the water that has filtered through the earth contains very little "free" oxygen. The worm has to come out to breathe. But earthworms are very sensitive to strong light, and just one hour in sunlight kills them.

Earthworms otherwise come out only at night. Then they stretch the front part

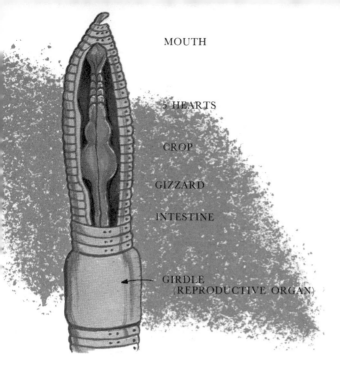

MOUTH

5 HEARTS

CROP

GIZZARD

INTESTINE

GIRDLE
(REPRODUCTIVE ORGAN)

of their body out of the hole. With its mouth the worm will grasp leaves and other plant material and pull the food down into the burrow to eat it.

Earthworms are hermaphrodites. This means that each worm is both a male and a female. When two earthworms mate, they press the front part of their bodies together. As they do that, they exchange sperm cells, which are deposited in a special little hollow in the skin. Later, when the earthworm is ready to lay eggs,

a special segment that is much thicker than the other segments starts producing a thick mucus, or slime. This forms a ring that slides over the head of the worm. As it slides forward, eggs are deposited in the ring, and the sperm cells are released into it also. As it slips off the worm completely, the ends of the ring close to form a sac-like container for the eggs. Inside, the sperm fertilizes the eggs, which then develop into small worms.

In winter many earthworms will dig themselves down deep into the ground, where the earth is warmer. Often dozens of worms will spend the winter together in a deep burrow, twisted together to keep each other warm.

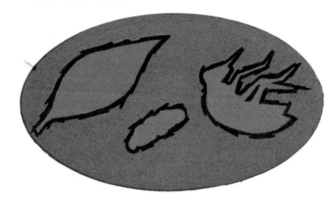

Food: vegetation, grubs, dead insects

FERTILIZATION TAKES PLACE   FERTILIZED EGGS

Mucus ring with eggs moves over head of worm, ultimately forming a cocoon

COCOON CONTAINING EGGS

Common Starfish

Asteria rubens

Starfish are related to sea urchins, sea cucumbers, and sea lilies.

There are about one thousand different kinds of starfish. The common starfish has five arms. Other kinds of starfish have more arms.

The mouth of the starfish is in the centre of its undersurface. From here the five arms stretch out in each direction. The starfish has a skeleton. This consists of little plates that lie right underneath the skin. On many of them are spikes

Food : oysters, clams, mussels

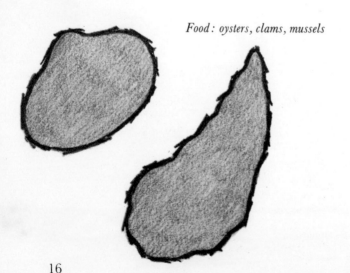

that help to protect the starfish. Starfish breathe through small pouches that stick out between the spikes. They are called skin gills. Around each skin gill is a ring of little pincers called *pedicellaria*. They keep dirt and small animals away from the skin gills. On the underside starfish have hundreds of little tubes, which are filled with water. With the help of small muscles the starfish can stretch each tube out and pull it back in. At the tip of each tube foot there is a little suction cup with which the starfish can hold onto things very tightly. Each tube foot is not very strong by itself, but when many work together, they can be very strong. The starfish uses its tube feet for crawling slowly over the rocky bottom of the shallow sea in which it lives. At the tip of each arm is a small light-sensitive spot that works like an eye. Inside each arm are parts of both the stomach and the sex glands.

When the starfish comes across a mussel or oyster, it will attack it. The mussel or oyster will close its valves with

*Starfish prises clam apart.
It everts its stomach into the clam
and so digests it*

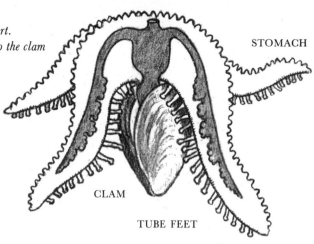

STOMACH

CLAM

TUBE FEET

its strong muscle. Then the starfish will put two arms on one of the valves, three on the other, and start to pull them apart. It may take it the whole day to overcome the strength of the oyster. But slowly the oyster tires and has to open its two valves.

Development of starfish

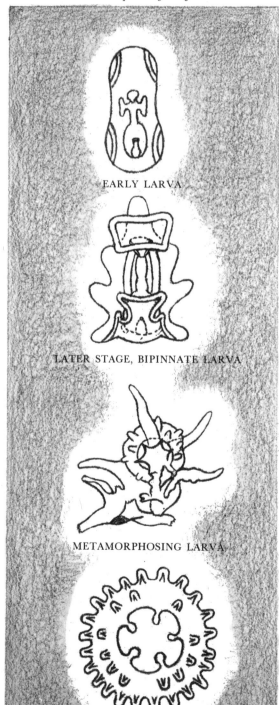

EARLY LARVA

LATER STAGE, BIPINNATE LARVA

METAMORPHOSING LARVA

SPINES DEVELOPING ON YOUNG STARFISH

Then the starfish folds its stomach inside out and sticks it in between the valves. The stomach juice dissolves the oyster and the starfish sucks up this partly digested food for further digestion. When it is finished, the starfish folds its stomach back into place and starts looking for another oyster or mussel to eat.

In spring the starfish releases either eggs or sperm. The sperm fertilizes the egg in the water, and in the course of a day or so a tiny larva is formed. It is elongated and has little hairlike cilia that help it to swim. After swimming about for a while, the larva falls to the bottom, where it attaches itself to a stone. While on the bottom it changes its shape to that of an adult starfish. The common starfish can grow to be 28 centimetres (11 inches) from the tip of one arm to the tip of the one opposite. If a starfish loses an arm, a new one will grow in its place.

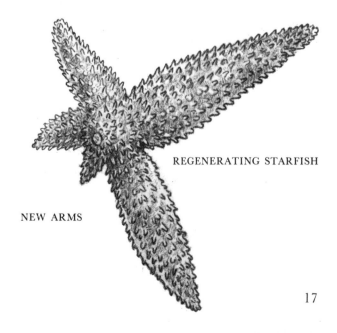

REGENERATING STARFISH

NEW ARMS

17

Octopus

Octopus vulgaris

The octopus and the squid are strange animals indeed. Scientists put them together in a group called *Cephalopoda*. *Cephalo* means "head" and *poda* means "feet", so the name can be translated as "animals with feet on their heads", which describes them very well. The octopus has eight arms, or tentacles, round its mouth. (Octopus is Greek for "eight feet".) On each tentacle are two rows of suction cups with which the octopus can seize and hold prey. It uses its arms for crawling along the bottom of the sea and for grasping crabs and molluscs, on which it mainly lives. When it has taken hold of a crab, the octopus brings it to its mouth

and crushes it with its strong, parrot-like beak. The octopus can also secrete saliva that is poisonous to the crab.

The octopus lives in caves and holes on the bottom of the sea. Here it lies in wait for crabs and fish. It has two large eyes and sees very well. Its skin can change colour like that of a chameleon, so that it can be very difficult to see. The octopus moves by shooting out a stream of water, and can propel itself quickly backwards or forwards—in other words, it is "jet-propelled". The octopus sometimes ejects a squirt of ink that makes the water murky and difficult to see through. Under cover of this "smoke screen" the

SUCKER DISC (TENTACLE)

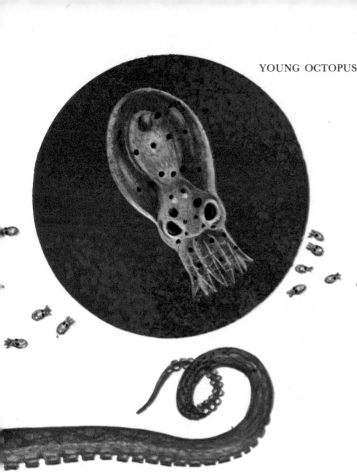

YOUNG OCTOPUS

STRINGS OF EGGS
HANGING FROM UNDERWATER
CAVE CEILING

octopus has a good chance of escaping its enemies.

When it is time to lay eggs, the male seeks out the female octopus. One of his eight arms is uniquely adapted for placing sperm in a special pocket in the female. When the female lays her eggs, she releases the sperm at the same time, and the eggs become fertilized. The eggs are laid in long clusters in the cave where the female lives. While the eggs are developing, the octopus keeps the water circulating over the eggs by her movements. She eats any larger animals that might be attracted to the eggs. In these ways the eggs live long enough to hatch. When they hatch, the larvae emerge. The larva looks like a very tiny octopus, and except for growing much bigger it really does not change shape. The common octopus grows to over one metre (4 feet) long. Its tentacles are a metre (3 feet) long. In the deep oceans there are other kinds of octopus that grow much bigger, with tentacles that can be more than 3 metres (10 feet) long.

When swimming, the octopus shoots a jet of water from its siphon to propel it forward or backward

Food: lobsters, clams, fish

Common Periwinkle

Littorina littorea

Snails are related to the oyster and the octopus. They are found in the sea, on beaches, on dry land, and in lakes and rivers.

The common periwinkle lives at the edge of the Atlantic Ocean both in Europe and North America. In some areas hundreds of them may be found attached to rocks and piers. When the tide leaves part of the beach dry, the snail retires into its shell. Its opening is closed by a hard plate on the upper side of its back. Before it closes itself in, the snail secretes a slimy juice with which it attaches itself to the rock. In this way the snail protects itself from drying out. It can remain alive for more than three weeks without being in the water.

The common periwinkle lives on the microscopic plants that cover the rocks and sand along the beach. Its tongue is covered with rows and rows of strong, sharp teeth, which gradually get worn away. But the tongue is very long, more than 5 centimetres (2 inches), and as the tip is worn off, the tongue protrudes just a little more. The tongue is curled up in a spiral in the snail's mouth.

The periwinkle moves at a speed of about 3 metres (10 feet) per hour.

The snails mate in the early summer. The male has a long mating organ that he inserts into a special pocket underneath the female shell. Here the sperm is deposited. After about twelve hours the female lays the first clutch of approxim-

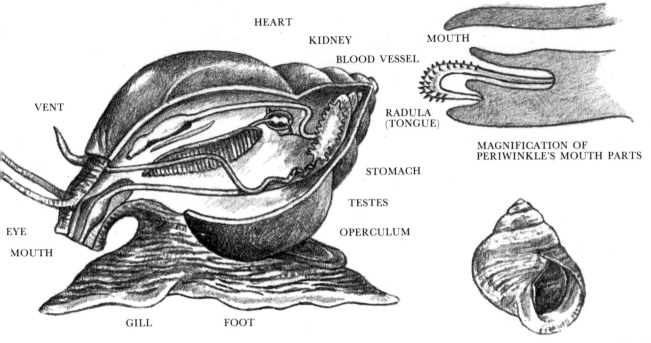

Anatomy of a periwinkle

HEART

KIDNEY

MOUTH

BLOOD VESSEL

VENT

RADULA
(TONGUE)

MAGNIFICATION OF
PERIWINKLE'S MOUTH PARTS

STOMACH

EYE

TESTES

MOUTH

OPERCULUM

GILL   FOOT

OPERCULUM (HORNY COVERING USED TO
PROTECT ANIMAL WHEN IN SHELL)

ately two hundred microscopic eggs. The eggs are enclosed in a flat capsule of a jelly-like substance that protects them. The female may lay about five thousand eggs during the summer. After six days the eggs hatch, and the larvae appear. The larva looks very different from the adult snail. It has no shell yet, but it has two flaps that it uses for swimming about. In the course of about four weeks the larva— called a veliger at this stage—changes to look like a small edition of the adult snail. Its body starts rotating by one side not developing as the snail grows. The spiral shell begins to form, and in the end the veliger loses its ability to swim. It settles on the bottom and now lives like the adults. When it is one year old, the periwinkle is mature and ready to mate. Although most periwinkles live to become only three years old, some can live as long as twenty years. Although they continue to grow a little throughout their lives, periwinkles do not become more than about 2·5 centimetres (one inch) long.

EGG MASS OF PERIWINKLES (MAGNIFIED)

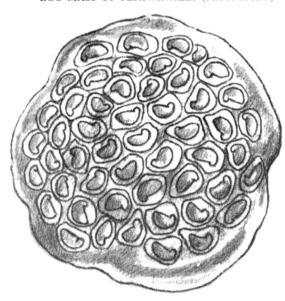

Food: algae

21

Oyster

Ostrea edulis

The oyster is the invertebrate most valuable to man. Invertebrates are animals without backbones. Every year thousands and thousands of oysters are caught or, in some cases, cultivated along the coastlines of the world.

As well as being good to eat, oysters form pearls, from which beautiful and costly jewellery is made. If a grain of sand is caught in the innermost part of the oyster's shell, the oyster forms a substance, mother of pearl, around the grain of sand. As the shell grows, the pearl grows larger with it.

Oysters are bivalves—this means they have two shells. The shells are formed by two lobes of the mantle, which is a soft tissue that covers the oyster like a coat. Inside the mantle is the rest of the animal, which consists of the heart, the digestive tract, where the food is absorbed, and the reproductive organs, from which come eggs and sperm. The oyster has no head and no mouth. The two shells are held

FREE-SWIMMING LARVA OF
OYSTER (VELIGER)

VELIGER LARVA OF OYSTER
(CLOSE-UP)

1 YEAR

3 YEARS

FULLY GROWN

22

together by elastic-like hinges. These would keep the shell open if it were not for a strong muscle which the oyster uses to shut the two shells tightly together.

Oysters live on the bottom of the sea where the water is not very deep. They cannot move. An oyster gets its food by opening its shells and letting water flow through, filtering from the water the tiny plants that it eats.

In the early part of summer the female releases her eggs–and there may be millions of them–into the water. At the same time the male releases sperm, which fertilizes the eggs. When the egg hatches, it is first shaped like a top. After two days it changes shape and looks like a tiny jelly-fish. The shell starts forming at once, but for two weeks the oyster swims freely in the water. It then falls to the bottom and its shell attaches to a stone or other hard surface. At this time it is only half a millimetre in length; in three years it grows to be nearly 80 millimetres (3 inches). It can grow to 300 millimetres (12 inches) and live to be twenty years old. Of the many millions of eggs only a few grow to be adult oysters. Most are eaten by crabs, fish or other animals. When the oyster has released its eggs, or spawned, it changes from a female to a male. It can then change and become a female again.

Even though oysters have to be in salt water to live and grow, they can survive for a long time after they have been taken out of the water. They keep their shells closed so that the water inside does not flow out. In this way they can live for two months on dry land. When the oyster dies, its muscle relaxes, and the shell opens up.

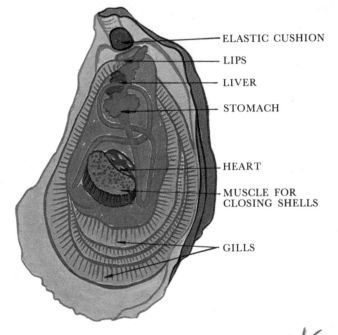

ELASTIC CUSHION
LIPS
LIVER
STOMACH

HEART
MUSCLE FOR CLOSING SHELLS

GILLS

Starfish prising open oyster shell

Lobster

Homarus vulgaris

Although quite closely related to the crab, the lobster looks and behaves quite differently. Both crabs and lobsters belong to a group of animals called decapods, which means "animals with ten legs". This species of lobster lives along the coasts of Europe and North America, where it is caught in traps. In summer, lobsters come in closer to the shore and that is when most of them are caught. They spend the winter farther out to sea in deeper water. Lobsters crawl on the bottom of the sea on their long legs, but they can also swim. Attached to each of the segments that make up the tail are two fan-like feet called swimmerets. By flapping them, the lobster can swim forward. By bending its tail suddenly, the lobster can swim backwards like a shrimp.

The lobster has two eyes, but it does not see very well. Much more important are the antennae with which the lobster feels its way. It has hair on the antennae by means of which it can hear. Lobsters can also smell. They smell the bait that fishermen put in their traps.

The lobster has two very large claws which it uses to seize fish and other prey. The claws are also fearful weapons with which the lobster can defend itself.

As the lobster grows, it forms a new shell to fit its larger size. This process is called moulting. Usually the lobster eats the shell it has shed. In this way it gets the calcium and other minerals necessary to make the new shell hard. When the time comes for a female to moult, a male will seek her out. A few hours after she has moulted, and while the new shell is still very soft, they will mate. The male

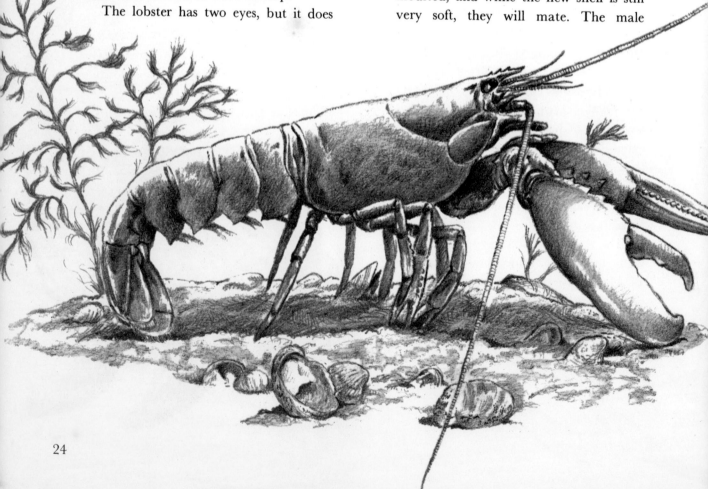

24

ZOEA OF LOBSTER
(NEWLY HATCHED)

YOUNG LOBSTER

Female carrying eggs on underside

places its sperm in a little pouch, the sperm receptacle, on the underside of the female. Here she carries the sperm until she is ready to lay her eggs. When she lays the eggs, the sperm is also released and fertilizes the eggs. The female carries the many thousands of eggs attached to the underside of her tail. She carries them for almost a year before they hatch. The lobster larvae look like shrimp and swim about on the surface of the sea. They moult several times before they sink down to the bottom and start their adult life.

Some lobsters reach a weight of 16 to 18 kilograms (35 to 40 pounds). Such a lobster is about 60 centimetres (2 feet) long and probably at least fifty years of age. The claws alone can be up to 50 centimetres (20 inches) long. That is almost as large as a football.

Food: carrion, detritus

Lobster trap

Fiddler Crab

Uca pugilator

The fiddler crab of the eastern coasts of America derives its name from its large claw. The female has two small claws, but the male has one small one and one large one, which is coloured a beautiful pink in the mating season. During this stage of reproductive activity the male waves the large claw up and down while in his burrow. This attracts the female and at the same time keeps other males out of its burrow.

Fiddler crabs live at the water's edge on tropical seashores. They build burrows in the sand. The burrows can be up to one metre (3 feet) deep. There the fiddler crab hides when there is danger, and there it stays when the tide comes in and buries the entrance to its hole. Only when the tide has rolled back does the crab come out of its hole. Then it searches along the beach for the tiny animals that were trapped by the sand as the tide receded.

In April, when the female fiddler crab is ready to lay her eggs, she becomes responsive to the male waving his big claw. When the crabs mate, the sperm is placed in a special pocket on the underside of the female. When she lays her eggs, the sperm is released and fertilizes the eggs. The female then carries the several thousand fertilized eggs attached to her underside until they are ready to hatch. Then she goes down to the water's edge and releases the young into the water.

The young look very different from the adult crabs. They are barely one millimetre long and look like little shrimps. At this stage the baby crab is called a zoea. Zoea means "life", and the zoea is lively indeed. It swims about near the surface of the water. Here it eats a lot of plankton—the minute plants and animals found floating in the sea. As the zoea starts to grow, its hard covering becomes too small for it, and a new covering forms under-

Courtship dance,
female on right

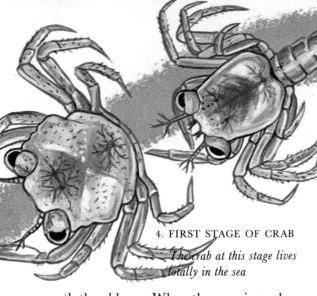

Development of fiddler crab

1. EGG

2. ZOEA

3. MEGALOPS

4. FIRST STAGE OF CRAB
The crab at this stage lives totally in the sea

neath the old one. When the zoea is ready to shed the old covering it swims to the bottom, where it lies motionless while the old covering breaks. When the zoea has pushed its way out, it swims back to the surface and starts eating again. All in all, it changes its covering, or it moults, four times. Each time it grows a little larger. After about one month it is twice as big as when it was hatched. Then the zoea moults again, but this time it looks different when it breaks through its old covering. It has now become a megalops, which means "big eyes". The eyes are truly large, and the front of the body is covered by a large shell, almost like that of a full-grown crab, but behind it is a tail like a shrimp's. It has long antennae in front with little hairs with which it feels and hears. For about one month the megalops continues to swim about and

eat and grow. Then, gradually, it loses its ability to swim and sinks to the bottom, where it finds a place to hide. Here it moults again, and this time it comes out looking like a little crab. As it grows, it moults again, and it lives like an adult fiddler crab except that it is not mature enough to breed.

When winter comes, all the fiddler crabs disappear into their burrows. Here they stay all winter in a deep sleep – they hibernate. Not until spring do they come out of their holes again. The young fiddler crab is now mature and ready to breed and have young of its own.

Fiddler retreats to sand tunnel in times of stress

Food: microscopic algae and plankton

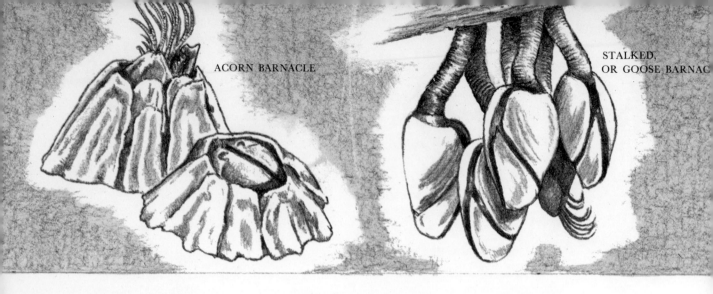

ACORN BARNACLE

STALKED, OR GOOSE BARNAC

Barnacles

There are many different kinds of barnacles. Two common kinds are the stalked, goose, or ship's barnacle (*Lepas fascicularis*) and the acorn barnacle (*Balanus balanoides*).

The stalked barnacle attaches itself by a long stalk to seaweed, logs, or other floating things. The body is enclosed in valves, as is a mollusc. The shell of the valves can grow to be up to 5 centimetres (2 inches) long. For a long time barnacles were thought to be molluscs (shellfish) because of their valves, but they really belong to a completely different order of animals. They are closely related to shrimps, lobsters and crabs, and with

them belong to a group of animals called crustaceans.

The stalked barnacle gets its food with the help of featherlike feet with which it brushes microscopic animals and plants into its mouth.

The acorn barnacle looks like a little volcano, with a tiny "crater" on top that can open and close. When the hole is open, the feathery feet emerge and brush food into the mouth of the barnacle. When the shell is closed, the barnacle is very well protected from its enemies.

Barnacles are hermaphrodites. This means that each individual is both a male and a female, and each has both male and

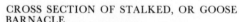

CROSS SECTION OF ACORN BARNACLE

CROSS SECTION OF STALKED, OR GOOSE BARNACLE

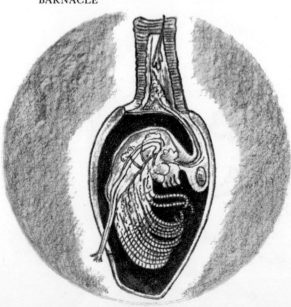

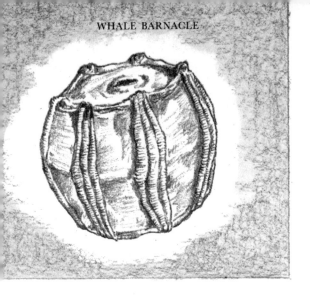

WHALE BARNACLE

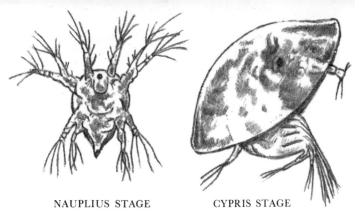

NAUPLIUS STAGE   CYPRIS STAGE

Young of acorn barnacle

Whale barnacles seen on whale

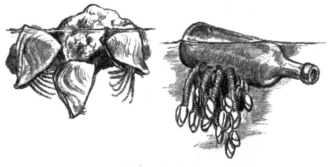

Barnacles floating on debris

Acorn barnacles seen at tide line

female sex organs. When the eggs hatch, a whole cloud of microscopic larvae swim away from the barnacle. Each tiny larva can swim well and forms part of the plankton that floats near the surface of the sea. It eats the microscopic plants found in the plankton. Soon the larva changes to the cypris stage. At this time it looks like a real barnacle, except that it swims about. But as soon as it finds a rock, or boat, or log, it attaches itself to it and becomes a true barnacle. Inside its shell a barnacle looks like a shrimp standing on its head, kicking food into its mouth.

Some kinds of barnacles, related to the acorn barnacle, attach themselves to sea turtles, whales, or even lobsters, and in this way are carried far and wide.

When barnacles attach themselves to the bottom of a ship, the ship becomes much heavier. Therefore the ship has to be taken onto dry land every so often to have the barnacles scraped off. Modern ships are now covered with a kind of plastic to which the barnacles cannot attach themselves.

Food: plankton

MALE

Garden Spider

Araneus diadematus

Spiders belong to a large group of animals called arthropods. Arthro means "joint" and pod means "leg", so they are animals with jointed legs. The lobster, crab, horseshoe crab, and all insects are arthropods. Arthropods do not have an internal skeleton. They are "kept together" by their hard skin. Muscles inside this hard skin, and flexible joints, enable the animal to move.

Food: insects

The garden spider has eight legs (insects have only six). Its body is divided into two parts. At the tip of the back part are six silk glands. These glands produce a liquid that turns into silk as soon as it comes into contact with the air. By varying the fluid the glands can produce different kinds of silk. As the silk is produced, the spider holds the thread free with one of its legs.

When the garden spider spins its web (and it spins a new one almost every night), it starts by making a bridge line. This line is strengthened by the spider before it starts to make a frame. Walking round on the frame it spins the radial threads that go from the centre to the edge of the frame. Next the spiral threads are spun; and lastly, the spider spins a thread leading from the web to a place nearby where it can hide.

Drops of sticky substance on web

The web can be more than a metre (several feet) across, although most are much smaller. Even newborn spiders make webs, but they are hardly larger than a postage stamp.

When a fly or other insect flies into the web, the vibrations are felt by the spider in its hiding place. It runs over to the web, and if the victim is a large insect, like a grasshopper, the spider spins a thread to tie it up. It then bites the insect and injects a poison into it. The poison paralyzes the insect so that it cannot move. The spider then sucks out the inside of the insect. Even though spiders have a good appetite, they can survive without food for more than a year.

When ready to mate, the male seeks out a female and puts his sperm into a special pocket in the female, and there the sperm lies until the eggs are ready to be fertilized. Sometimes the female catches and eats the male after they have mated.

*Newly hatched spiders cling
together in a ball and let
themselves down to the ground
on a fine web*

The female lays from three to eight hundred eggs in a cocoon she has spun with her silk. The eggs lie until spring, when they hatch, and a new generation of spiders comes out. The female dies soon after the eggs are laid.

The garden spider lives for only one year, but other kinds of spiders may live to be over twenty years old.

*1. Spider throws out bridge line on the breeze
2. Radial threads being added to structure
3. Completed orb web*

31

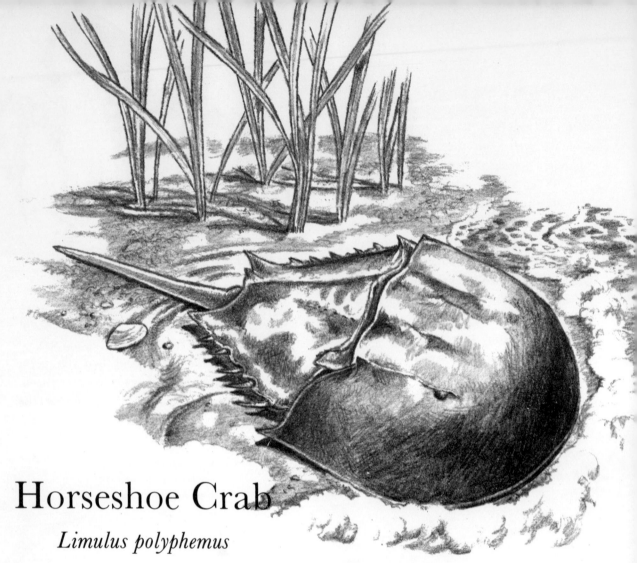

Horseshoe Crab

Limulus polyphemus

The horseshoe crab is not a crab at all. The nearest relatives of the horseshoe crab, or king crab, as it is also called, are spiders and scorpions.

The horseshoe crab has no separate head. Instead, its head and chest form one large part called the cephalothorax (which means "head-chest"). Behind the cephalothorax is the abdomen and behind that is the long, sharp tail. The horseshoe crab has five pairs of legs that end in small pincers. The sixth pair of legs has no pincers. In the centre of the cephalo-thorax, on the underside where the legs meet, is the mouth. The horseshoe crab has no special muscle or teeth in its mouth for chewing food – worms, mussels, plants, and other things it finds on the bottom. Instead, the innermost part of each leg has long spines that grind up the

food when the horseshoe crab moves its legs.

Horseshoe crabs spend most of their time on the bottom of the sea not too far from shore. They can also swim, using, like oars, six pairs of flattened appendages. Sometimes they will swim to the surface upside down. When they let themselves fall to the bottom again, they can turn over with the help of their long tail.

Horseshoe crabs have two pairs of eyes. One pair is set wide apart on the top of the cephalothorax. The other pair is set close together at the front end of the cephalo-thorax.

In spring horseshoe crabs come in close to shore. The males, which are smaller than the females, will seek out their mates. When a male has found his female, he will hang onto her shell with his feet. One day, when the tide is low, the pair will crawl ashore. The female digs a hole in the sand, where she lays the eggs, which are then fertilized by the male. Then the parents crawl back into the sea.

A couple of months later the eggs hatch. The young horseshoe crab does not look much like its parents, but more like an animal that lived millions of years ago, the trilobite. However it changes to look

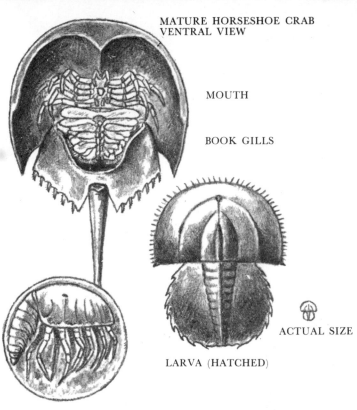

MATURE HORSESHOE CRAB
VENTRAL VIEW

MOUTH

BOOK GILLS

ACTUAL SIZE

LARVA (HATCHED)

TRILOBITIC STAGE
(SHORTLY BEFORE HATCHING)

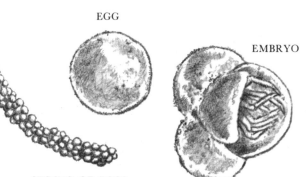

EGG

EMBRYO

STRING OF EGGS—
EGGS ARE ABOUT 3 MILLIMETRES ($\frac{1}{8}$ INCH)

like a small horseshoe crab. As it grows the horseshoe crab moults frequently. Its cast-off shells are often found on the shore.

Horseshoe crabs grow slowly, sometimes to a length of 50 centimetres (20 inches). One species is found along the eastern coast of North America and four other species in Asia. They do not occur in Europe.

Stages of growth of embryonic horseshoe crab (magnified)

Possible ancestor of horseshoe crab

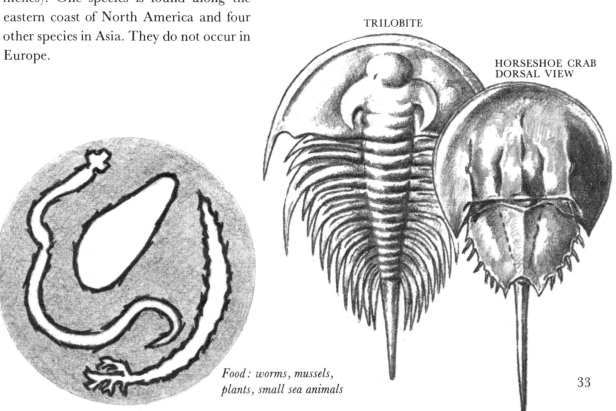

TRILOBITE

HORSESHOE CRAB
DORSAL VIEW

Food: worms, mussels, plants, small sea animals

33

Monarch Butterfly

Danaus plexippus

Butterflies are among the prettiest of insects. Their colourful wings and fluttering flight are so characteristic of summer that everyone knows them. There are many kinds of butterflies. More than one hundred thousand different species inhabit the world.

The monarch butterfly is one of the most widespread. It was originally found only in North, Central and South America, but has now spread to both Europe and Asia.

The monarch starts as a tiny egg that the mother lays on the underside of a milkweed plant. It is a pale green colour and looks like a drop of dew. After about four days the egg hatches and a tiny caterpillar appears. It first eats its eggshell. Then it eats its way through the leaf. For the next two weeks the caterpillar (striped black, green, and yellow) does hardly anything but eat. It has very strong jaws with which it cuts off little pieces of leaf. As the caterpillar grows, it sheds the skin that no longer fits its larger size. All in all, it moults four times. After two weeks the caterpillar has grown to be 5 centimetres (2 inches) long. At this time it starts spinning a silken string underneath a leaf. The silk is formed by glands in the caterpillar's mouth. The caterpillar attaches itself to the string by its tail. It then encloses itself in a case of silk and gradually changes into a pupa. The case splits open and reveals a smooth, green pupa hanging by the silk string. Inside the pupa case the caterpillar changes into a butterfly in the next two weeks. Then the pupa case splits open and out crawls a fully grown monarch butter-

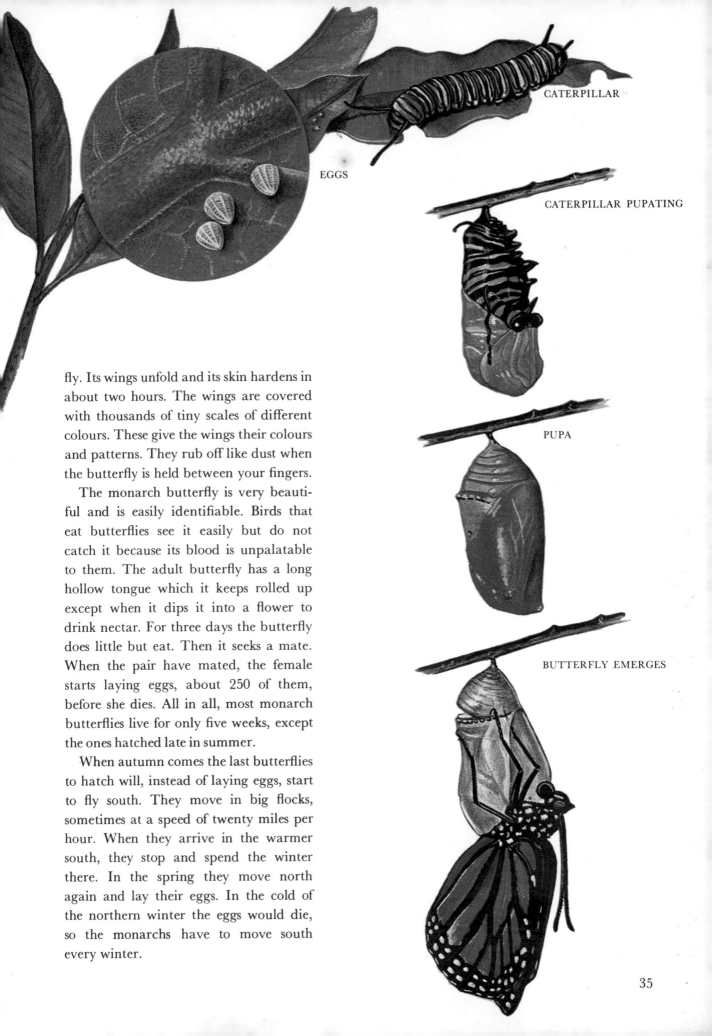

EGGS

CATERPILLAR

CATERPILLAR PUPATING

PUPA

BUTTERFLY EMERGES

fly. Its wings unfold and its skin hardens in about two hours. The wings are covered with thousands of tiny scales of different colours. These give the wings their colours and patterns. They rub off like dust when the butterfly is held between your fingers.

The monarch butterfly is very beautiful and is easily identifiable. Birds that eat butterflies see it easily but do not catch it because its blood is unpalatable to them. The adult butterfly has a long hollow tongue which it keeps rolled up except when it dips it into a flower to drink nectar. For three days the butterfly does little but eat. Then it seeks a mate. When the pair have mated, the female starts laying eggs, about 250 of them, before she dies. All in all, most monarch butterflies live for only five weeks, except the ones hatched late in summer.

When autumn comes the last butterflies to hatch will, instead of laying eggs, start to fly south. They move in big flocks, sometimes at a speed of twenty miles per hour. When they arrive in the warmer south, they stop and spend the winter there. In the spring they move north again and lay their eggs. In the cold of the northern winter the eggs would die, so the monarchs have to move south every winter.

Dragonfly

Odonata

There are many different kinds of dragon-flies, but all lead about the same kind of life and all have long, broad wings and long, slender bodies. They are most commonly seen near water. The young dragonflies (called larvae or nymphs) live underwater.

The female lays her eggs in the water of a shallow pond. She may lay as many as one hundred thousand eggs. A large number of these eggs are eaten by fish and other animals, but some hatch into nymphs. The nymph is a pencil-thin insect. On its six legs it crawls about on the bottom of the pond or among the plants that are found there. When it gets close to another insect, a mosquito larva

UNDERWATER NYMPH

LARVAL FOOD

ADULT FOOD

for instance, the nymph shoots out its lower lip, or labium, and grasps its prey. The lower lip is then retracted and the nymph places the mosquito larva in its mouth and eats it.

The nymph breathes with the help of gills. Gills are for many water insects what the openings in the skin are for air-breathing insects. With the gills, through which the air canals run, the animal can extract oxygen from the water just as our blood extracts oxygen from the air through our lungs. The gills in the nymph are found in the lower end of its intestines. The nymph can push the water out through this opening so fast that it swims forward with a sudden jerk. This rocket-like propulsion helps protect it from its natural enemies.

As the nymph grows, it moults many times, and it eats bigger and bigger prey. It even eats small fish. After from one to

three years the nymph is ready to change into a real dragonfly. It crawls out of the water and attaches itself to a reed. While it sits there, it changes to a dragonfly. The skin breaks, and the real dragonfly emerges. Its damp wings stretch out and in an hour or two they are dry enough to allow the insect to fly. Dragonflies can move their beautiful, glistening wings twenty-five times per second and can fly at a speed of 80 kilometres (50 miles) per hour. In the air they catch with their legs other insects, mosquitoes in particular, and kill them with their strong jaws. In autumn the dragonflies die, but nymphs still live in the water and are ready to emerge as dragonflies the following year.

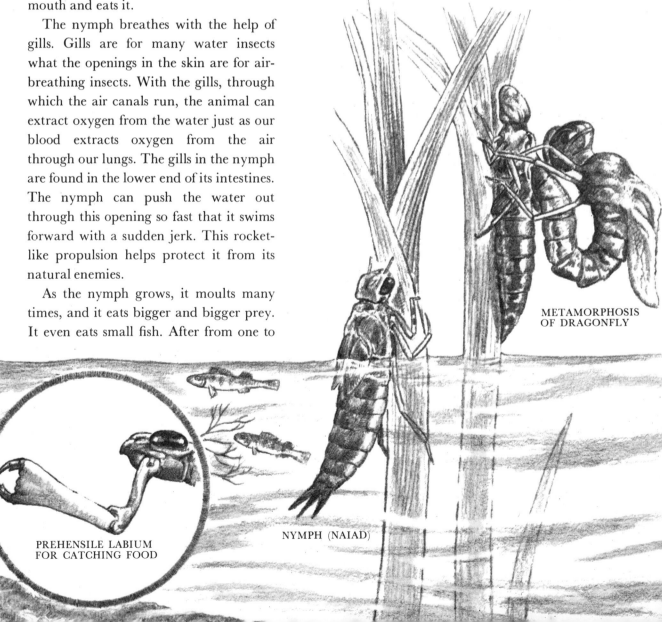

METAMORPHOSIS OF DRAGONFLY

PREHENSILE LABIUM FOR CATCHING FOOD

NYMPH (NAIAD)

Migratory Locust

Locusta migratoria

There are many different kinds of grass-hoppers and locusts in the world. Like other insects, the grasshoppers have no skeleton. Instead, they have a stiff, strong skin that protects them and gives support to their internal parts. All insects have three pairs of legs. Insects breathe through openings in their protective skin. These openings bring oxygen into all the different organs that need it.

Some insects look very different from their parents when they are young. They are larvae. When they are ready to become adults they protect themselves inside a pupa. Here they change completely until they become like the adult insect. This is called a complete metamorphosis.

Other insects, like the migratory locust, look like their parents when they are born. When the locust eggs hatch, the locust looks like a very small locust except that it has no wings and its head is large. It is called a nymph. It has two large jaws with which it bites off little

Head of migratory locust

38

Food consists of all vegetation in the path of locust hordes. Where crops have been devastated by locust plagues, famine results

pieces of the plants that it eats. After four weeks the wings start to grow, and when it is eight weeks old, it is adult. From birth it has very strong hind legs and it can jump over a metre to avoid its enemies.

Some kinds of male grasshoppers have a row of little thorns on the inside of the thighs of the hind leg. They rub the thorns against a vein in the wings and produce the "song" that can be heard on summer nights. Other kinds of male grasshoppers produce a song by rubbing the first pair of wings together. The song attracts the female, and when the male and female have mated, she starts laying eggs. She slides the end of her body into the ground

and deposits a clump of about one hundred eggs there.

The migratory locust, which lives in Africa, sometimes produces an oversupply of nymphs. When they grow up, they are overcrowded and it is then that they start wandering in large swarms. The flocks may contain thousands of millions of locusts. They travel at a speed of about 15 kilometres (10 miles) per hour and eat everything in their path. They cause great damage to crops in the lands they pass through. Although the wandering locusts can produce two generations per year, the migrating flocks eventually die out. But, as they have done for centuries, others will follow, from time to time.

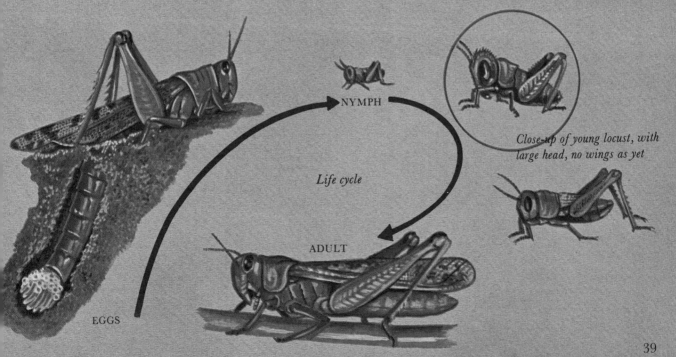

NYMPH

Close-up of young locust, with large head, no wings as yet

Life cycle

ADULT

EGGS

Honey Bee

Apis mellifera

The honey bee has been kept by man for several thousand years. Because of this, it is the insect we know the most about.

Bees live in colonies, usually in a hollow tree or box. New colonies are started by old ones. When a wild honey bee colony becomes overcrowded, the queen and some workers leave together and fly to a hollow tree where they start to build a new colony. Some bees collect sap from trees. They carry it home in a sort of basket that is formed by hairs on their hind legs. In the nest other bees secrete wax from some glands on their bellies. The sap and the wax are mixed and used to close all the cracks and holes in the nest.

The wax alone is used for building cells. Each cell is oblong with six sides. The cells are built side by side, and layer upon layer, so that they form an upright comb. Here the honey is kept, and here the eggs are laid.

The queen, who is the only bee in the colony who lays eggs, mates once and sometimes twice in her life. She leaves the colony, and while flying, mates with a male. The male dies, but his sperm has been put into a special pocket and the queen can release the sperm when she starts laying her eggs. She returns to the colony after her nuptial flight to lay two kinds of eggs. One kind, the fertilized eggs, develop into workers or queens, while the other kind, which are unfertilized, become males or drones. Special cells have to be made for the eggs that will develop into queens. These cells are

40

Food: nectar from flowers

of a different shape from the rest, and when the larva emerges it is fed exclusively with a special food, "royal jelly", secreted from the workers' stomachs. The other larvae are fed pollen and honey which the workers collect from flowers and store in the cells. About the ninth day after the egg is laid, the larva forms a pupa and the cell is sealed up; at about the fifteenth or sixteenth day a full grown bee emerges. For the first few days the young bee cleans out cells and helps to incubate the larvae. After four or five days it is old enough to feed the larvae and, finally, when twelve days old, it is ready to make and repair cells. Only when the bee is about three weeks old does it leave the hive and fly in search of food—nectar, pollen and water. In the stomach of the bee the nectar is changed into honey. Most worker bees live for only six weeks. The males do not work, their only function being to mate with a queen. The queens that hatch are either killed by the old queen, or if she has left the colony, the new queen will kill the other queens as they hatch. Each nest, even though it may consist of fifty thousand workers, has only one queen.

When a worker returns to the hive with nectar and pollen, it dances vigorously in a pattern. This dance tells the other bees the direction and distance where flowers may be found.

Bees also have the ability to sting. At the end of their body is a needle-sharp pin. The pin is hollow and contains a stinging poison. When the bee stings something the needle falls off, leaving a wound from which the bee dies.

In winter, honey bees cluster together in the nest. In the centre is the queen, who is kept warm by the other bees.

EGGS (MAGNIFIED)

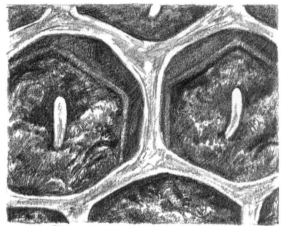

LARVAE

QUEEN

WORKER   DRONE

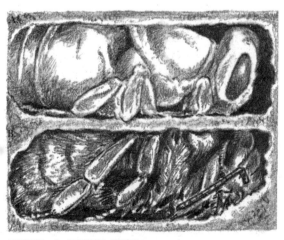

ABOVE: A. WHITE PUPA
B. YOUNG BEE

41

Ants

Formicidae

Ants are found almost throughout the world. There are many different kinds of ants, but most lead lives that are quite similar.

Ants live in colonies. These colonies are mostly underground. There may be as many as a million ants in a single colony. There are three different kinds of ant: queens, males, and workers. The workers are the most numerous, and they do not have wings.

The queens and males have wings, but they use them only once, at the time of mating. At this time hundreds of queens and males leave the colonies and start their mating flight. They mate in the air.

When the male alights, he soon dies, but the queen usually starts a new colony. Her wings are bitten or rubbed off as she has no more use for them. She digs a hole in the ground and starts laying eggs. When the eggs hatch the queen feeds the larvae, small white grubs, until they are ready to form pupae. The pupae, or cocoons, are formed by fine threads the larvae secrete from glands in their mouths. The larvae spin the cocoons in such a way as to completely surround themselves. These cocoons are often called "ant eggs", but they are not really eggs at all. After two or three weeks the larva has changed into an adult. The older ants have licked the cocoon and moved it about, which makes it possible for the ant to bite its way out of the cocoon. When it emerges the ant is ready to take part in the work of the colony.

After the first workers have emerged from their cocoons, the female does nothing but lay eggs. Some workers seek food and bring it back to the nest. Others

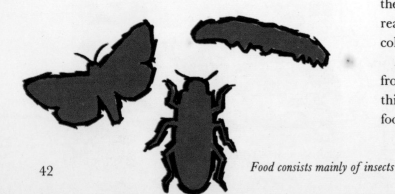

Food consists mainly of insects

stay in the nest and care for the eggs, larvae, and cocoons; while others build the nest bigger. Each nest consists of many galleries and chambers, all interconnecting. Eggs, larvae and cocoons are kept in separate compartments with the queen in a chamber of her own at the centre of the nest.

Different kinds of ant eat different kinds of food, but most eat other insects and dead animals. Other ants are "farmers"; they take advantage of the fact that aphids – small, fat insects that live on leaves and trees – secrete honeydew. The ants collect honeydew, much as the farmer collects milk from cows.

Several queens can lay eggs in the same nest, but when mating time comes the young queens and males fly off to start new colonies. In winter, the ants cluster together in the deepest part of the nest, and here they sleep throughout the winter. When summer comes, they go back to work. A queen may live for fifteen years; the workers live for a much shorter time, about seven years.

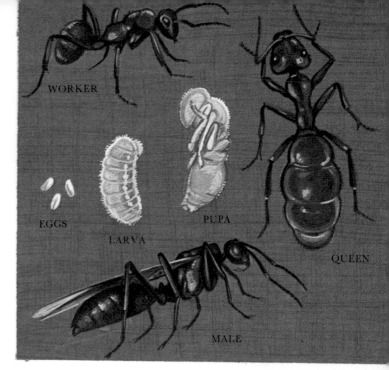

Members of wood ant colony

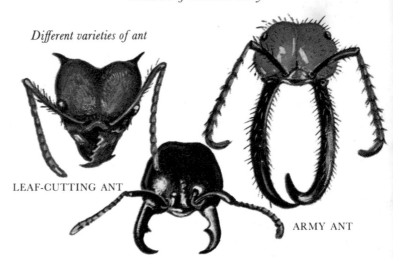

Different varieties of ant

LEAF-CUTTING ANT

ARMY ANT

BLIND SOLDIER OR DRIVER ANT

Nest (mound) of wood ant

Pine needles and twigs form the outer covering of mound

The mound is built so as to catch and hold the warmth of the sun

Soil piled above ground

The tunnels are chambers used to hatch and rear young

Fish are the most primitive of all the vertebrates (animals with backbones). Fish all live in water. There are thousands of different kinds of fish. They are divided into two big groups, the ones that have skeletons of pliable cartilage, such as sharks, rays and skates, and the bony fish that have skeletons of bone. Most fish are bony fish. Although cartilage fish are the most primitive and came into being before the bony fish, many of them have survived until the present day.

One of the biggest of the cartilage fish is the great white shark. The great white shark is also called the man-eater, because it sometimes attacks people.

The great white shark, like most fishes, is streamlined and can move fast—at a speed of about 40 kilometres (25

Great White Shark

Carcharodon carcharias

Food: seals, sea lions.
Sharks eat people only incidentally

UPPER TOOTH   LOWER TOOTH

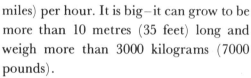

miles) per hour. It is big—it can grow to be more than 10 metres (35 feet) long and weigh more than 3000 kilograms (7000 pounds).

The great white shark spends most of its time far out at sea, swimming near the surface looking for food. Almost anything that looks edible will do. It has even attacked boats. Mostly, though, it lives on fish and sometimes on other sharks, sea lions, and seals. When pursuing its prey, the shark may dive very deep. Some have gone down to more than 1000 metres (4000 feet) below the surface, where the sun cannot reach and it is completely dark. Sharks have poor eyesight but a keen sense of smell, with which they locate their prey. A wounded animal attracts a shark because of the smell of its blood. Sharks breathe with gills, as do other fish. Their gill openings are not covered. These are the five rows of slit-like openings one can see right behind the head of the shark.

Scientists know very little about the mating habits of the great white shark. Most sharks mate by the male planting his

seed into the female with a special organ. The great white shark gives birth to live young. They are over one metre (50 inches) long when they are born. They are ferocious animals, as are their parents. Their teeth are very sharp, and they have many of them. Sharks' teeth grow in rows inside the mouth. Such a row of teeth is sharp enough to cut a big fish like a tuna in two in a single bite. The teeth are really a special kind of scale growing on the skin of the mouth. The skin scales of the shark are like thorns, hard and sharp, and they do not cover the shark skin com-

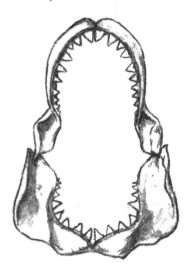

JAW OF MAN-EATER (WHITE SHARK), 84 CENTIMETRES (33 INCHES)

pletely, as the scales of other fishes cover them. The great white shark has to be nearly 4 metres (about 13 feet) long before it is mature and ready to mate. It is a dangerous animal then, and many careless people have been eaten by great white sharks.

Cod

Gadus morhua

Cod are found throughout the North Atlantic. Like all fish, they are covered with fine scales. The scales grow mainly in summer, and growth rings are formed on the scales like the rings in trees. This helps us determine the age of a cod. Cod can be found at a depth varying from about 2 to 300 metres (6 feet to 1000 feet). Here they live on herring, mackerel, and other fish. The mouth of the cod is large and strong, and it has very sharp teeth. Cod can swim at a speed of about 25 kilometres (15 miles) per hour. They swim by moving their body from side to side so that the tail flaps strongly, propelling them forward.

Other fins are used for stabilizing the fish in the water.

The cod, like all fish, breathes with the help of gills. At the sides of the mouth there are slit-like openings through which water flows. Inside the gills are many small blood vessels. The blood takes oxygen from the water and gives off carbon dioxide. Like other fish, the cod has an air bladder in its body to give it buoyancy in the water.

In late winter cod start assembling in the spawning areas. Here the females lay their eggs, and the males release their sperm. This is called spawning. One

GILL FILAMENTS

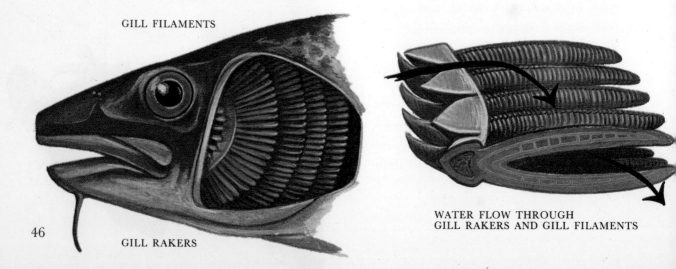

GILL RAKERS

WATER FLOW THROUGH
GILL RAKERS AND GILL FILAMENTS

Development of cod

1. EGGS

Food: shrimp, fish, shellfish, squid

2. NEWLY HATCHED

3. LARVA, TWO OR THREE WEEKS OLD

4. YOUNG FISH, SIX MONTHS OLD

female can lay up to five million eggs. The sperm fertilizes the eggs in the water. The eggs then drift to the upper layers of the water. After three to four weeks they hatch, and the young cod, no more than 6 millimetres ($\frac{1}{4}$ of an inch) in length, start swimming about in the plankton. Here they live on shrimp and other small animals. Millions of these young fish are themselves eaten by other fish and sea birds; others die when the current carries them to parts of the sea where the temperature is either too high or too low. But many survive and grow. After about three months they have grown to be 50 millimetres (2 inches) long. They then go down to the bottom of the sea. There they live on small crabs, shrimps, and worms. As they continue to grow, they start eating fish. When the cod is about five years old, it has reached a length of about 68 centimetres (27 inches) and is ready to breed. With other cod it then seeks out the spawning areas. Cod can become very large. They can weigh up to 90 kilograms (200 pounds) and reach a length of about 2 metres (6 feet).

Cod-fishing banks off New England

Common Eel

Anguilla vulgaris

The eel is a long, slender, snakelike fish. The adult eel lives in the fresh waters of both Europe and North America. It is well suited for wriggling among the plants and through the mud of the bottom. It eats almost anything living within reach— mussels, snails, worms and fish. It becomes very fat. Then, rather suddenly,

Food: fish, mussels, worms, snails

the eel becomes restless and one autumn night it leaves the pond or lake where it has spent most of its life. It travels very slowly (about half a mile per hour) and will, if necessary, leave the water and travel overland to reach the sea. After about six months it finally arrives at its spawning grounds in the Sargasso Sea. This "sea", very rich in plankton and floating seaweeds, lies in the Atlantic Ocean off Bermuda, more than 3000 kilometres (2000 miles) from the European coast. Here the females lay their eggs, and the males release their sperm. After this the adult eels, both male and female, die.

The eggs float in the water at a depth of about 400 metres (1300 feet). It is possible for the eggs to stay at this depth because they contain small oil drops that prevent them from sinking to the bottom, nearly 5000 metres (15,000 feet) below, or floating to the surface above. When the larva emerges it is only 6 millimetres ($\frac{1}{4}$ of an inch) long. It is flattened from side to side and does not look like an eel at all. It moves to the surface of the water, where it lives on shrimps and other tiny animals found in the plankton. Slowly it swims and drifts towards the European waters. The journey takes about three years, by which time the eel has grown to 76 millimetres (3 inches) long. It then changes to become like the adult eel, snakelike in shape. When it reaches a pond or a lake, it settles there for perhaps nine to twenty years before it returns to the sea to spawn and die. The Sargasso Sea is the spawning

Eels on their way to the sea can travel from one waterway to another

ground for European and American eels.

Eels that have been kept in captivity have lived to be fifty years old, but they have never bred.

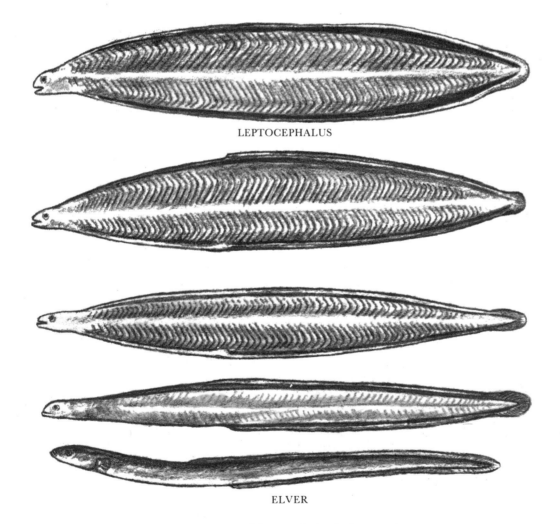

LEPTOCEPHALUS

ELVER

Metamorphosis of eel

Atlantic Salmon

Salmo salar

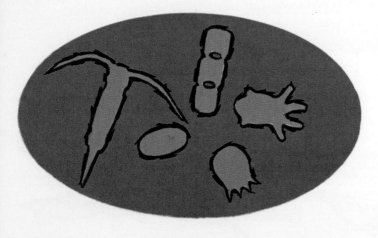

Food: plankton

The Atlantic salmon is found on both sides of the Atlantic, in North America as well as in Europe. It starts its life in early spring in a small river or brook. For the first five to six weeks it lives mainly on the yolk that is still attached to it. The young salmon is then known as an alevin. When the yolk sac disappears, the fish is known as a parr. The parr stays in the brook. Here it lives on small insects, snails, and other animals. When it turns to silver and is about 20 centimetres (8 inches) long, it is called a smolt. The smolt travels down the river and into the sea. In the sea the salmon grows very fast during the summer. It lives on the shrimp and squid found in plankton. Some of the animals it eats contain the same substance that gives carrots their orange colour. When the salmon eats them, the colour substance, which is called carotene, is deposited in the flesh. This is what gives salmon meat its reddish colour.

In the plankton the salmon finds plenty of food. It grows very fast. Some may put on as much as half a kilogram (one pound) of weight per month. Some may grow to weigh as much as 22 kilograms (50 pounds). The salmon stay out at sea for about four years before they start travelling back to the streams where they were hatched.

As soon as the salmon reaches fresh water, it stops eating. It starts swimming

Female laying eggs, male fertilizing them — showing the breeding colours

against the current of the river. When it comes to a waterfall, it tries to jump over it. It is this habit that has earned the salmon its scientific name, *Salmo salar*, which means "leaping salmon". It sometimes takes the salmon a whole year before it reaches its home stream. Each stream has its own characteristic chemical composition and the salmon usually returns to the stream of its birth or one of similar odour.

When the salmon swims up the stream, it stops at a shallow part where the bottom is covered with gravel. Here the female digs a hole 10 to 15 centimetres (4 to 6 inches) deep. While she is doing this, a male also stops at the same place. He does

not help her dig, but chases other males away. When the female is ready to lay her eggs, the male comes up and lies alongside. Exactly at the same time that she lays her eggs he releases his sperm. The eggs become fertilized, and the female now covers them with gravel, which protects the eggs. She then moves on and digs another hole in which to lay more eggs. She continues this until she has laid all her eggs in the gravel.

After spawning most salmon are so exhausted that they die. Only a few make it back to the sea, to return to the spawning grounds the next year. Salmon can, at most, spawn four times and live to be thirteen years old.

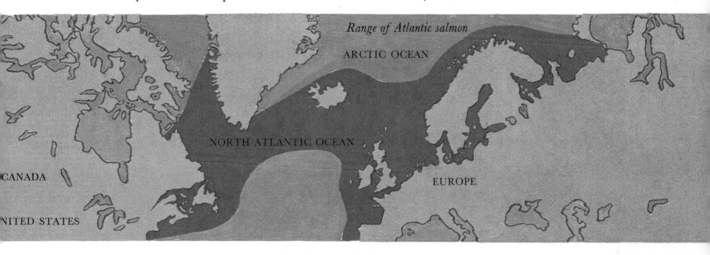

Range of Atlantic salmon

ARCTIC OCEAN

NORTH ATLANTIC OCEAN

CANADA

UNITED STATES

EUROPE

Development of salmon

EGG   YOLK   ALEVIN   PARR

FEMALE

Seahorses are among the most remarkable of fishes. For one thing, they do look a little like horses, and even the scientific name *Hippocampus* means "horse-caterpillar". They are found along warm-water coasts, always in salt water. A seahorse has a long tubelike snout and, unlike most other fish, can swim in an upright position with the head bent forward. It has no tail fin, but the tail is long and flexible and is used for holding onto seaweed. Seahorses are covered with bony plates that help to protect them from their many enemies. It is this bony covering that one sometimes finds on the beach after all the inside of the dead seahorse has disappeared.

The common seahorse is found along the Atlantic coast of America. It varies in colour from almost white to red or blue. It is about 12 to 20 centimetres (5 to 8 inches) long. Each eye of the seahorse can move independently. In this way the seahorse can keep an eye on everything going on about it. Most of the time it spends hanging onto a strand of seaweed with its tail. It can swim, but only slowly, by flapping its fins more than thirty times per second. The seahorse does not catch its prey by chasing. It lives on the minute shrimp which it sucks into its tiny mouth. It is so accurate in its suction that no shrimp less than 5 centimetres (2 inches) away can avoid it.

The breeding habits of the seahorse are very strange in that the female lays her eggs in a pouch on the male's belly. As

Common Seahorse

Hippocampus hippocampus

Head-on view of pouch of male "mother" showing young ready to be born (variety zostera)

MALE

they enter the pouch the eggs are fertilized. The female lays about twenty-five eggs. The male keeps the eggs in the pouch for ten days or so, until they hatch. Then he delivers the baby seahorses from the same opening through which the eggs were deposited. The newborn are only about 12 millimetres ($\frac{1}{2}$ an inch) long, but they grow quickly. In four months they are 76 millimetres (3 inches) long, and after ten months they have grown to full size. Seahorses eat a lot. They may eat more than three thousand baby shrimp in just one day. Most seahorses do not live very long; they are eaten by other fish before they become adults. Even those that do reach adult size live only for two to three years.

Food: minute crustaceans

Common Frog

Rana temporaria

The common frog is an amphibian. "Amphibian" means an animal that is equally at home in water and on land. Toads and newts are also amphibians. Amphibians were the first animals that left the water millions of years ago to spend some time on land. Amphibians still show their close connection with water by spending at least a part of their lives in it.

The common frog is the best known of all amphibians. Like other amphibians, it has a smooth skin without scales, and it has no claws. Like other frogs, it has strong hind legs. In the water it swims and dives well. On land it can either crawl or jump. In one jump it can cover over a metre (45 inches). This is quite impressive when you remember that it is only a small animal of 10 centimetres (4 inches) long. It avoids danger by jumping, and if it can, it will

jump right into the water of its pond.

The common frog lives on slugs, invertebrates, worms, and insects. It has a very special way of catching them. When it spots a fly or other insect, it waits until

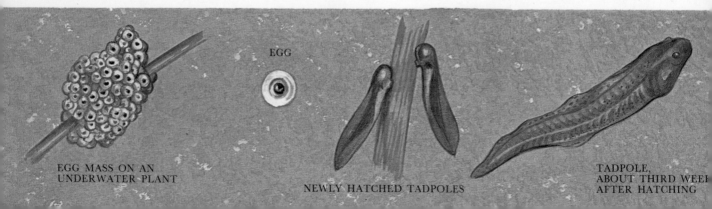

EGG MASS ON AN
UNDERWATER PLANT

EGG

NEWLY HATCHED TADPOLES

TADPOLE,
ABOUT THIRD WEEK
AFTER HATCHING

Food: crustaceans, snails, slugs,
butterfly larvae, earthworms

Common frog
laying its eggs
in water

the prey is close by. Then it suddenly throws out its long, sticky tongue. The tongue is so sticky that the insect cannot free itself.

In spring frogs leave the meadows and other comparatively dry places and move to ponds and water holes where the males start croaking to attract the attention of the females. When they croak, two large balloons appear, one on each side of the head, giving the croak its deepness of tone. There are very few differences in the appearance of male and female common frogs, and the male frog will frequently clasp any frog smaller than itself, even other males. The male frog usually responds with a loud harsh croak, and the male that made the mistake lets go. When a female comes near, the male grasps her under the front legs with his front legs and holds on until she has laid her eggs. As she lays her eggs in the water, he releases his sperm, which fertilizes the eggs. The eggs, three to four hundred of them, form a large clump of jelly-like foam. Here the tadpoles develop. After four days the egg hatches, and the tadpole comes out. It is a very different looking animal from the grown-up frog. It has no legs, but it has a long tail which it uses for swimming about. It lives on microscopic plants and grows very quickly. Slowly its legs start to grow, and its tail disappears. After sixty days it has grown to look like an adult frog. It then leaves the water and starts eating insects like the adult.

When the weather becomes cold, the frog goes back to the water. Here it hides under stones or in mud, sometimes with several hundred others, and hibernates. When spring comes it wakens up and returns to the meadows.

DPOLE
TER SEVENTH WEEK,
ND LEGS FORMING

TADPOLE,
AFTER TENTH WEEK,
LEGS FORMED, TAIL DISAPPEARING
OUT ON LAND

YOUNG FROG

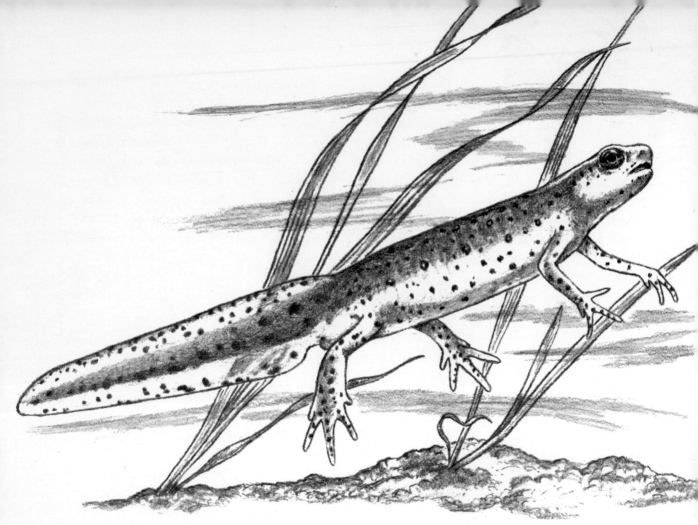

Newts

Triturus

Like frogs, newts are amphibians, though they differ in many ways. The most striking difference is that they have tails, whereas frogs are tailless.

In general, newts look more like lizards, though lizards are reptiles. Reptiles, such as lizards, snakes, turtles, and alligators, have scales and claws, both of which are missing in the newts.

Most newts spend more of their life in water than frogs and reptiles do.

One of the best known species of newts in North America, Europe and Asia is the common, or smooth, newt which grows to about 102 millimetres (4 inches) long. Both male and female are greenish-brown above with reddish-brown spots along the sides. The underside is yellow. The tail is flattened from side to side.

The common or smooth newt spends most of the year on land, returning only to the water in the breeding season. It is

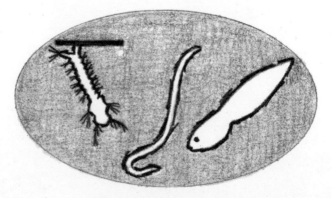

Food: worms, insect larvae
small aquatic animals

56

the least aquatic of our newts. During the day it hides under the cover of stones, emerging at night to prey on the small insects, worms, molluscs and other animals it feeds upon. In early spring the male starts courting the female. He lays a clump of sperm in front of the female. She picks it up in her cloaca. The cloaca is the cavity that the intestinal, urinary, and genital tracts open into in amphibious and several other animals. Here the sperm remains until the eggs are fertilized. When the female starts laying the eggs, each one attaches itself to a leaf or stem growing in the water. Inside each egg the young newt grows for four to five weeks, then it breaks out. It looks very much like an adult newt, but is a great deal smaller. On each side of the head are the gills with which it extracts oxygen from the water. For three to four months it spends all its time in the water, eating other small animals and growing. It then changes into a eft. This eft looks very much like a lizard and spends all its time on land. Here it stays hidden under logs and stones in moist woods. It lives on worms and insects. For two to three years the eft stays on land. In winter it hibernates, well hidden in the moist ground. After two to three years it starts changing colour. It becomes darker and more like the adult in appearance. It then returns to the water, and not until then is it ready to breed.

Stages in development of newt

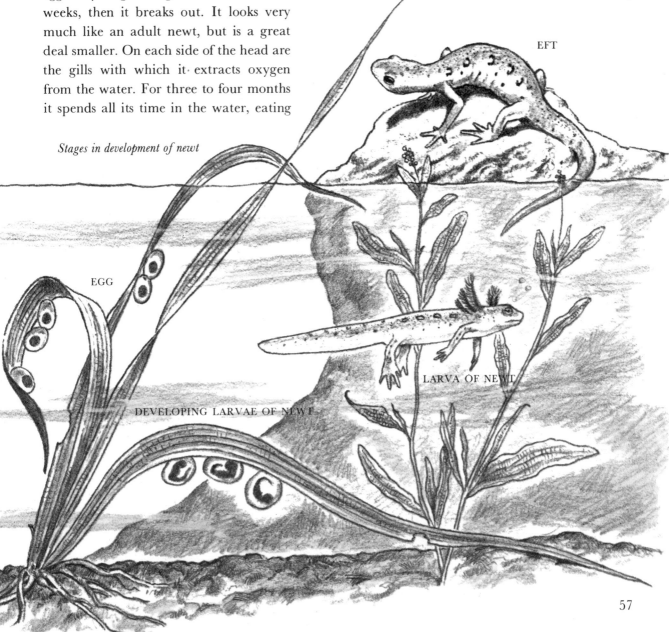

EFT

EGG

DEVELOPING LARVAE OF NEWT

LARVA OF NEWT

Tortoise

Testudo

Tortoises and turtles, or terrapins, are reptiles. Other reptiles are lizards, snakes, and alligators. The dinosaurs, which lived more than fifty million years ago, were also reptiles.

The name for this reptile varies from country to country but mostly we reserve turtle for the aquatic form (sea-water and freshwater varieties), and tortoise for the land-based animal. The tortoise we know is mainly a plant-eater but some kinds eat insects, as well as various fruits and berries. It also likes mushrooms and can eat even the poisonous ones. In the wild each tor-

toise has its own territory in which it spends its whole life. Usually the territory is about 225 metres (750 feet) in diameter. The Eastern Box Turtle can live to be very old. The oldest one that we know about was 138 years of age.

Old tortoises have shells. The top shell, or carapace, is formed by the ribs. On top of this bony shell is a horny shell that keeps growing back as it is worn down. Covering the underside is the lower shell, or plastron. Between the two shells the head, legs, and tail stick out. But the tortoise can, when it wants, pull them all in underneath the shell. The shell is very strong and protects the tortoise from its enemies. The tortoise has no teeth, but it can bite with its horny bill.

In early summer the mating season starts. When a male and female tortoise meet, he courts her by bobbing his head up and down. He might even give her a friendly bite on the head. When the tor-

58

Food: mushrooms, berries, worms, insects, vegetation

toises mate, the male crawls up on the shell of the female and swings his tail underneath hers. The lower shell of the male is curved inwards so that he does not slide off her top shell.

After mating, the female lays about six eggs in a hole approximately 7 centimetres (3 inches) deep. Usually she has chosen a sunny spot where the eggs can be kept warm. After ten to sixteen weeks the baby tortoise breaks through the soft shell of its egg. It then has to take care of itself. Its shell is about $2\frac{1}{2}$ centimetres (1 inch) long. It grows slowly, and when it is

Shell of tortoise closed for its protection

five years old, the shell is 7 centimetres (3 inches) long. Not until it is twenty years of age has it reached 12·5 centimetres (5 inches) in length.

Tortoises are very slow animals. They walk or crawl at a speed of only 150 metres (500 feet) per hour. If they feel threatened, they will immediately retreat into their shell. When they do that, they give a gasp to let the air out of their lungs. This gives them sufficient space to pull themselves into the shell.

In autumn the tortoise finds a protected spot where it digs itself down and hibernates. Throughout the cold months of the winter it sleeps protected by its shell. When the warm spring comes, it crawls out of its hole in the ground and continues its daily life.

Tortoise hatching

Yolk sac on lower plastron of newly hatched tortoise

Eggs of tortoise buried beneath soil and vegetation

Eastern Diamondback Rattlesnake

Crotalus adamanteus

Many snakes are harmless. Not so the rattlesnake, and particularly not the Eastern diamondback rattlesnake. It is the largest of all rattlesnakes, growing to about 2·5 metres (8 feet) in length, and is one of the most dangerous snakes in the world.

It is dangerous because its bite is poisonous. The rattlesnake has two special teeth, or fangs, in its upper jaw. They are long, sharp, and hollow. If one is destroyed, the rattlesnake quickly grows another. Most of the time the fangs rest in two grooves

in the mouth. When the rattlesnake bites, it thrusts the fangs through the skin of the victim, injecting a poison that is produced by a gland behind the fangs. The poison destroys the blood and paralyses the victim.

Rattlesnakes use their poison to kill the animals they eat. As snakes cannot chew their food, they have to swallow their prey whole. Because they have very flexible skeletons, they can swallow prey that is much larger than themselves.

Rattlesnakes find their prey–rabbits,

rats, mice and birds—with the help of their sense of smell and their sense of heat. When a snake flicks its tongue in and out, it is smelling its surroundings. The tongue brings the smell into the mouth where the sense organs are. Rattlesnakes have two little hollows, one on either side of the face, that are sensitive to heat. Even in the dark a rattlesnake can find and kill its prey with the help of this sensitivity.

Snakes have no legs. They move about by winding their bodies over the ground. The scales on the underside grip the surface of the ground and push the snake forward. Rattlesnakes move at a speed of about 3 kilometres (2 miles) per hour. Since rattlesnakes eat such big meals, they need eat only about once a week and can go for many weeks without food.

Rattlesnakes mate in summer. While the female and male wind round each other, the male releases his sperm into the female. The female is pregnant for two to three months, then she gives birth to about ten young, each of them about 30 centimetres (12 inches) long. As soon as it is born, the young snake looks after itself. As it grows—and it continues to grow almost its whole life—the snake sheds its skin about once a year. All the skin except the tip of the tail is shed. The pieces left on the tail form the "rattle". When the rattlesnake gets excited, it moves its tail rapidly, causing the pieces to rattle. This might frighten enemies away. When it is about two years old, the rattlesnake is mature and ready to mate. It can live to be twenty years old.

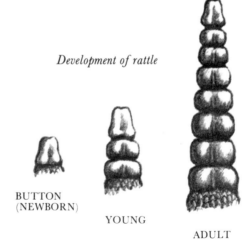

Development of rattle

BUTTON (NEWBORN)

YOUNG

ADULT

Food: rabbits, birds, mice and rats

POISON GLAND

Cutaway drawing of head of rattlesnake showing hollow fangs and poison gland

61

American Robin

Turdus migratorius

Different from the European bird of the same name is the beautiful American robin – common in gardens and woods throughout North America. Like all animals, it has a scientific name. This is a name in Latin that is the same throughout the world. In this way all scientists know which animal they are talking about, even if they do not know the name in the different languages. The American robin's scientific name is *Turdus migratorius*. *Turdus* means it is a thrush and *migratorius* shows that it migrates. Migration means that the animal at some time moves away from an area, only to return later. The American robin migrates to the southern and warmest part of North America in the winter when snow and ice cover the

ground in its summer areas. When spring comes, the robins start flying north in large flocks. They fly both by day and by night in a straight course, even in adverse weather conditions.

When the male robin arrives at a suitable nesting place, he settles down. Soon he starts to sing. His song serves two purposes. First of all it tells other male robins where he lives, and warns them to stay away from the area he considers as his territory. If another male robin comes within this territory, he will be chased away. The song also attracts a female robin whom the male courts.

Soon the female starts building a nest in a tree, a bush, or on a ledge. The nest consists of an outer layer of coarse twigs and

grass and even little pieces of cloth. Inside, the robin makes a deep cup of mud that hardens and makes the nest very strong. The cup is then lined with fine grass.

Now the robin starts laying eggs. She lays one egg every day for four days, when the clutch is complete. She keeps them warm by lying on them. Inside each pretty blue egg the embryo—the unborn young—grows, and after two weeks it starts breaking through the shell. When they are first hatched, the young are almost completely naked, their eyes are closed, and their mouths and bellies are very large. The female robin has to sit near the babies to keep them warm until their own feathers have grown out. The young birds grow very fast on the worms and insects they eat. The young robins do not have to learn how to fly. They can do so as soon as the feathers on the wings have grown out. The parents might feed them for a little while, but mostly they have to fend for themselves. They eat worms, which they see or hear moving about beneath the surface of the ground. They also take insects, and in autumn and winter, berries. In autumn, when the weather gets cold, they start flying south for the winter.

FEMALE ON NEST

ROBIN EGG

NEWLY HATCHED YOUNG

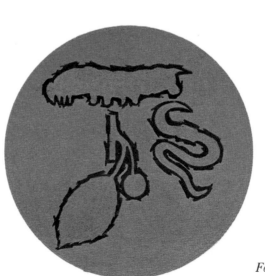

YOUNG ROBIN

Food : insects, fruit, worms

63

Ostrich

Struthio camelus

Ostrich foot

The ostrich is the biggest bird in the world. It can be up to 2·5 metres (8 feet) tall. It differs from other birds not only in its size but also by being unable to fly. We usually think the ability to fly is common to all birds, but some birds do not fly, and other animals, like bats and insects, do. It is really the feathers on birds that make them different from all other animals. The ostrich has wings, but they are very weak and cannot be used for flying. However it has two very long, very strong legs with which it can run very fast. Its speed has been measured at more than 48 kilometres (30 miles) per hour. This is important for the ostrich as there are many lions, leopards and other predators (animals that hunt other animals) on the African plains where it lives. Like antelopes and zebras, the ostriches try to outrun their enemies.

When it is time for breeding the male starts courting the female. He sits down in front of her with his wings and tail spread out showing the beautiful feathers. After

Ostrich egg, chicken egg, and hummingbird eggs, showing comparative sizes

they have mated, the female lays her eggs in a shallow hole in the ground. An ostrich egg is very large. It can weigh up to 1·25 kilograms (3 pounds), and it would take more than forty-five minutes to boil it. The shell is so large and so strong that it can be used as a cup if it is cut in half.

As in other birds the egg is formed in the sex gland called the ovary. At first it consists only of the yolk, which is yellow, and a tiny white spot from which the embryo develops. When the egg is released from the ovary, it passes into a long tube (the oviduct) where it is fertilized by the sperm. As it passes through the tube, the egg white is deposited round the yolk and the disc. When the white has been deposited, the egg passes into another part of the tube where a shell is formed round the whole egg. The egg then passes out of the female's body. The white spot has already started developing into an embryo. It grows very fast, getting its food from the yolk and the white. The shell is not completely airtight, and the embryo can breathe through the shell.

The ostrich lays ten eggs. During the night the male sits on them to keep them warm. During the day the female, who is brown and hard to spot, sits on them. Sometimes she leaves the eggs half buried in the sand and lets the sun keep them warm. After six weeks the eggs hatch. The young are completely covered with down and start following their parents about right away. They find their own food, which consists mainly of insects. The young are brown with dark spots, and they are very hard to see when they are lying still to escape danger. It takes the young three years to grow up.

Young ostriches hatching

Food: lizards, rodents, insects, vegetation

Cuckoo

Cuculus canorus

In Europe the arrival of the cuckoo shows that spring has really come. Over heaths and through the woods is heard the characteristic call of the bird—"cuck-oo". As in many other animals, the cuckoo's name is an imitation of its call. The cuckoo is about 33 centimetres (13 inches) long and has a very long tail. It is found in treeless areas and in woodlands, also on commons.

Food consists of insects, especially caterpillars

Most cuckoos are grey in colour, but for some reason unknown to scientists, some of the females are reddish-brown.

As soon as the cuckoo has arrived in the spring, it takes up a territory, as most other birds do. But the cuckoo does not build a nest of its own. Instead it seeks out smaller birds who are busy building their nests or who have already started laying eggs. From its perch on a wire or bush the cuckoo can see a considerable distance. When it has spotted a suitable nest it flies down to it, lays its own egg in the nest, and takes one of the other eggs in its bill. Sometimes it eats the other egg and sometimes it throws it away. The cuckoo's egg is very small, hardly any bigger than that of the smaller bird. Most birds of a certain species lay eggs that are all similar and special for their own kind. Not so with the cuckoo. Each female lays its own kind of egg. It looks like the eggs of the kind of bird in whose nest it is laid. In that way the little bird, who is called the host, cannot tell the cuckoo's egg from its own. Each cuckoo prefers to lay its egg in a special kind of host's nest. The host might be a pipit or a warbler or any other kind of bird.

Sometimes the little bird leaves its nest when a cuckoo has laid an egg in it but, usually, it continues to sit on the egg, together with its own, as if nothing had happened. Inside the cuckoo's egg the young develops and grows much faster

Meadow pipit feeding cuckoo
baby that it has raised as its own

than the young inside the eggs of the little bird. Thus the cuckoo's egg hatches first. The tiny cuckoo then starts getting rid of the other eggs. Although blind and naked, it is strong enough to get underneath one of the other eggs and heave it over the edge of the nest. It goes on doing this until all the eggs have been thrown out of the nest. In this way the cuckoo makes sure that its foster parents have only one to feed, namely itself. The cuckoo grows very quickly, and soon it is much bigger than its foster parents, who are even busier fetching food for the cuckoo than if they had a whole clutch of their own to feed. The cuckoo grows to such a size that the foster parents sometimes have to stand on its back to put worms and insects into its mouth. After about three weeks the cuckoo is big enough to fend for itself and it leaves its foster parents. Then it starts eating large hairy caterpillars, the favourite food of cuckoos. In late summer the cuckoos fly south to Europe and Northern Asia, where they spend the winter. The following spring they return to lay eggs in other birds' nests.

Newly hatched cuckoo quickly
ousts the other nestlings

Emperor Penguin

Aptenodytes forsteri

Besides the ostrich, there are several other birds that have lost the ability to fly. Famous among these are the penguins. There are many different kinds of penguins. Thousands of years ago there were penguins that stood five feet high. These big penguins became extinct a long time ago, and we only know about them from finding their bones. Today the largest living penguin is the emperor penguin. It is over one metre (45 inches) tall and weighs about 34 kilograms (75 pounds), or as much as a ten-year-old child. It is also the hardiest of all penguins, living off the coast of Antarctica, where it is very cold. In winter the temperature may drop to −56°C (−70°F).

Penguins cannot use their wings for flying. They are shaped like oars, and the penguins use them like oars when they swim. The emperor penguin, like all penguins, swims and dives very well. It often stays in the water for several weeks at a time. Its short feathers lie very close together, and underneath this waterproof coat is a thick layer of down that helps to keep it warm. The emperor penguin can swim at a speed of more than 40 kilometres (25 miles) per hour. At this speed it has no

Young penguins

trouble catching its food. Emperor penguins live mainly on squid. They can catch and eat squid that are up to 91 centimetres (3 feet) long. The stomach of a penguin is very large and can hold a lot of food, enabling the animal to survive for long periods without eating.

By May, which is autumn in the southern hemisphere, where Antarctica is, the emperor penguins have grown very fat. They clamber onto the ice and start walking and sliding on their bellies to the spot where they bred the year before. This spot is often dozens of miles from the open water. When the emperor penguins have reached it, they start their courtship, which lasts about three weeks. The female then lays a single egg, which the male takes and places on top of his feet. A large flap of skin from his belly covers the egg and keeps it warm. The females then leave the colony and go back to the open sea. It is now June, and the sun has gone down, not to rise again for several months. For nine weeks the males stand close together in the darkness and coldness of the Antarctic winter, keeping the eggs warm. Just as the eggs hatch, the females come back. They start feeding the tiny young, while the males go back to sea to eat for the first time in three months. They eat steadily

for about three weeks, then they return to the colony, and the females take off. So they continue for another three months, until one day all the penguins start to go back to the open sea. At this time the young have lost the downy plumage that protected them from the cold while they were small. Now they have waterproof plumage like their parents so that they can swim and catch their own food.

Keeping egg warm

At sea the emperor penguin has many enemies. Most feared are the Leopard seals with their sharp teeth, and the sharks. If the emperor penguin can avoid all these dangers, it can live to be more than twenty years old.

Penguin swimming

Food: squid, fish

69

Bald Eagle

Haliaeetus leucocephalus

The bald eagle is the national bird of the United States of America. It is a very beautiful bird, dark brown with a white head and neck and a white tail. It is one metre (40 inches) long. When it spreads its wings it is over two metres (90 inches) from wing tip to wing tip. The bald eagle is a strong flyer, but most of the time it soars. On its long broad wings it circles higher and higher. It sometimes flies so high that it is difficult to see it from the ground, even with binoculars.

Bald eagles mate for life. Male and female stay together until one of them dies. Then the one still alive takes another mate. Early in spring the bald eagles start re-pairing their old nest. The nest is usually placed high in a tree, sometimes more than 15 metres (50 feet) above the ground. As the same nest is used year after year, it can become very large. Some are over 3 metres (10 feet) high and 2·5 metres (8 feet) across. Such a nest weighs 1800 kilograms (4000 pounds). It is made of branches the eagles carry to the nest in their talons. The inside of the nest is lined with soft moss and grass. The nest is so big that other birds sometimes breed in the lower part of it. Even the great horned owl has been found building its nest in that of a bald eagle.

In the far north, where there are no tall trees, the eagles place their nests on rocks. When the nest is ready, the female lays two white eggs. Both male and female take turns sitting on ("incubating") the eggs. They incubate them for thirty-five days. Then the two baby eagles break through the shells. They are covered with white

Nests, found in high trees or rocky cliffs, are built of sticks and lined with weeds, feathers, moss, and grasses

Young eagles are covered with down

Eggs are white

down, but have the strong hooked bills of their parents. They stay in the nest for nine to ten weeks. When their first set of real feathers has grown out, they leave the nest. The young eagles are brown with whitish spots, and not until they are three years old do they get the beautiful dark brown and white colouring of the adult bird. They are then ready to find a mate and start breeding.

Bald eagles eat a variety of food. They can catch rabbits and ducks, but most often they eat fish which they find washed ashore; only rarely do they catch them in the water. Sometimes they attack ospreys (or fish hawks, as they are also called), and steal the fish they have caught.

Bald eagles used to be very common, but they have disappeared from many states. Their scarcity is the result of two things: before the birds were protected many were killed by hunters. Secondly,

the poisons used for killing insects get into rivers and are taken up by the fish eaten by the eagles. When the eagles eat the poison, they do not die, but the eggs they lay have very thin shells and break easily. Thus very few baby eagles hatch.

The bald eagle may live to be about fifty years old.

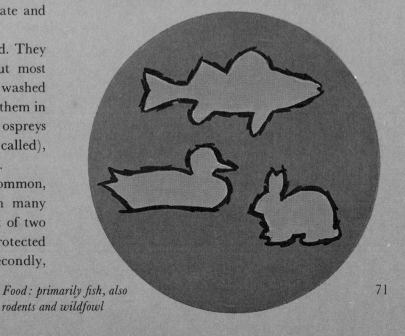

Food: primarily fish, also rodents and wildfowl

Platypus

Ornithorhynchus anatinus

The platypus is a mammal. Mammals are animals that have mammary glands to produce milk for their young. Like birds, mammals are warm-blooded. This means that they maintain a certain temperature in their body even when the surroundings are colder.

The platypus is a very primitive kind of mammal. It does not give birth to its young, it lays eggs like a bird. The mammary glands do not form a nipple, the milk is secreted onto the skin, and the young lick it off.

The platypus lives in swamps and along river banks in Australia. It catches tadpoles, crayfish, and other small water animals. Its mouth is formed like the bill of a duck; it has no teeth. Its feet are webbed, and its tail is flat, almost like a beaver's. It is a very good swimmer. When

alarmed the platypus will make a slapping sound on the water with its tail. It was long suspected that the animal did this and it has now been proved.

The platypus is a shy animal. It does most of its hunting at dawn and at dusk. The rest of the time it spends in its burrow in the bank of a river. The burrow can be very deep – some have been found to be 30 metres (100 feet) long.

During the courtship of the animals, which takes place before they mate, the male will sometimes hold onto the female's tail with his bill, and they will swim round in circles. They mate in the water. Soon after mating, the female disappears into a special burrow she has made. Here she has a nest filled with leaves. She lays two eggs, which she keeps warm until they hatch ten days later. The young are blind when they are born and do not open their eyes until they are eleven weeks old. They stay in the nest for about sixteen weeks. Even after they have started swimming about outside the burrow, they live on their mother's milk for another four weeks. Not until then can they fend for themselves. During all this time the male is not allowed near the young, and he has nothing to do with the family.

Food : crayfish, tadpoles, worms

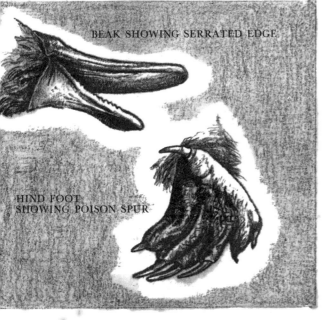

BEAK SHOWING SERRATED EDGE

HIND FOOT
SHOWING POISON SPUR

When the young are a year old, they are grown up and ready to mate. A platypus can live to be ten years old; throughout that time it uses the same burrow, except for breeding.

BABY PLATYPUS

In the underground nest of the platypus the eggs are attached to each other, as shown above

Red Kangaroo

Macropus rufus

Marsupials, or pouched animals, are mammals whose young go through most of their development in their mother's pouch. The opossum and the red kangaroo are both marsupials. The grey and the red kangaroo are the largest marsupials. The red stands 200 centimetres (7 feet) high and weighs 90 kilograms (200 pounds). Its hind legs are very strong, and so is its long tail, which it uses as a fifth leg.

Kangaroos often stand on their tail and hind legs alone, and when they fight they box with their front legs.

Kangaroos can move rapidly over the ground by leaping and jumping. They use their hind legs only, and can run at a speed of 50 kilometres (30 miles) per hour, covering 9 metres (30 feet) in one long jump.

Red kangaroos live in the hot, dry

scrubland of Australia. Here they move about in flocks, finding grass and leaves to eat. They spend the hot part of the day in the shade underneath trees and bushes. In the cool of the evenings they seek their food in the open.

Kangaroos mate once a year. The fertilized egg stays in the womb, which is a muscular cavity, for only four weeks. Its only nutrition is from the yolk sac. In other mammals a special organ, the placenta, develops in the womb of the mother. The growing foetus then receives its nutrition from the mother through the placenta. This does not happen in the marsupials; the young are born before they are completely developed. When the kangaroo is born, it is about 25 millimetres (1 inch) long, and only the front legs are well developed. The mother lies on her back when she delivers. With her tongue she has licked a path from the birth opening to the pouch. The newborn kangaroo takes about fifteen minutes to crawl along the path to the pouch. It then crawls into the pouch where the nipples are found, takes a nipple into its mouth and stays attached to it while it grows.

Food : vegetation

Australia is the only continent where kangaroos are found

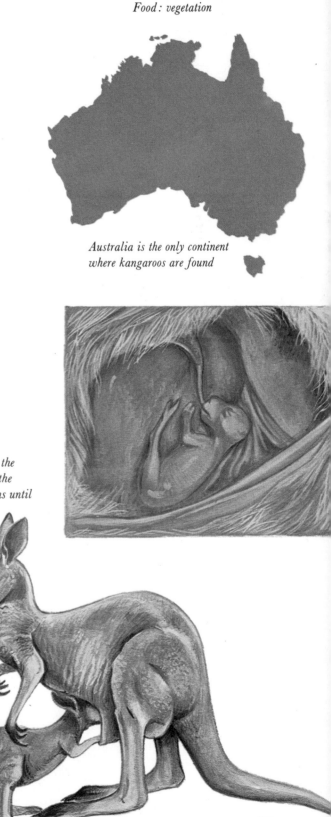

Once inside the pouch, the baby attaches itself to the nipple, where it remains until it is more mature

A kangaroo baby too large for the pouch still returns to its mother for protection and to nurse

Kangaroo baby still in pouch

75

House Mouse

Mus musculus

There are many kinds of mice. The most widespread is the house mouse. Since earliest times, when man started building houses and farming land, the house mouse has been with us. Where man has moved, the house mouse has moved along with him.

The house mouse is not very big. The head and body together are only a little more than 76 millimetres (3 inches) long. The tail is the same length; all in all, the mouse is 152 millimetres (6 inches) long. Like most mice, the house mouse prefers to stay hidden during the day. At night it comes out and seeks its food. It has big eyes and sees well at night. Its ears are also good. It has long whiskers with which it can feel things. The long tail is almost naked, and instead of hairs, it is covered with little scales.

The house mouse has very strong teeth. As in other rodents, the group of animals to which squirrels, beavers, rabbits, and mice belong, the front teeth keep growing throughout life. They are worn down and kept sharp by the upper and lower teeth grinding against each other. With their sharp teeth house mice can easily open up

Baby mice are born blind

nuts and chew their way through wood, and are even known to have gnawed holes in water pipes.

House mice eat almost everything they can get hold of – cheese, bacon, bread, and lots of other kinds of food.

Mother and young raid the pantry

When the female is about two months old, she is grown up and ready to have young. A male mouse fertilizes her eggs, which attach themselves to the inside of the womb, or uterus, as it is also called. As the eggs grow they get their food from the mother's blood through a special organ called the placenta. A new placenta is formed for each young. After about three weeks a litter of nine young is born. The young are blind and naked and helpless, but they grow very fast on their mother's milk. After about two weeks the eyes open and the fur begins to grow. It now takes only another two to three weeks before the young can fend for themselves. By that time their mother might already be about to give birth to another litter.

The house mice live in nests built of straw, cloth, and paper, in a hole or in a dark corner. Mice do not live very long, at the most a few years, for they have many

Food: everything a human eats

enemies, including cats, owls, hawks, and snakes. However, they come into breeding condition so quickly that there are always plenty of them about.

Beaver

Castor canadensis

There are beavers in the old world and the new. It is now accepted that they are geographical races of the same species, although the European beaver rarely constructs dams.

The beaver is the largest rodent found in North America. It is about one metre (3 feet) long and a large one can weigh up to 30 kilograms (70 pounds). The beaver has a flat, scaly tail, about 25 centimetres (10 inches) long and 12 centimetres (5 inches) wide. The beaver uses its tail for steering when it is swimming and for support when it is sitting upright on its hind legs. When the beaver is excited, it beats its tail on the water.

The beaver's front legs are small and are used only for holding things. The hind legs are very strong, and there are webs, little flaps of skin, between the toes, which help the beaver to swim.

Beavers live in streams or ponds where there are trees and bushes. They eat the bark of trees, leaves and twigs. They can easily gnaw through wood with their strong front teeth.

In autumn, beavers collect food for the winter. To get the bark they fell trees by gnawing all round the trunk until the tree

Food: aspen leaves, bark from poplars and aspens

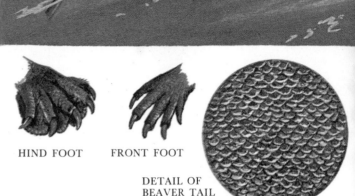

Beaver carrying food (a branch of aspen) to its underwater home

falls. They then gnaw the branches into pieces about 180 to 300 centimetres (6 to 10 feet) long. When that is done, the beavers drag the pieces down to the water. As they always go the same way, a neat path becomes hollowed out. They also cut canals on flat ground, making transport of the wood easier. The branches are carried underwater and rammed into the mud near the lodge. When the lake is frozen in winter, the beaver can get to this underwater food supply without having to go out into the open.

Beavers use the branches for other things besides food. They build a lodge in their pond, hollowing the inside for their burrow. This has several entrances, all opening underwater. To keep the water at

HIND FOOT   FRONT FOOT

DETAIL OF BEAVER TAIL

Beaver cutting a tree for its dam with its large front incisor teeth

the same level the beavers build dams of logs, mud and rocks. In winter the beaver does not have to go outside at all. It carries food from the underwater supply to its burrow, using the entrances under the ice.

In the middle of winter the male and female beaver mate. In May, the female beaver gives birth to between two and six baby beavers. They are covered with very soft hair, and their eyes are open when they are born. Very soon they start swimming about, playing all the time. Later, when they have grown bigger, they start working like their parents, felling trees and building dams. They stay in the pond for two years. They are then adult and leave the pond to find another one where they can start their own little family.

BEAVER HOUSE

TUNNEL FROM FOOD SUPPLY TO HOUSE

UNDERWATER FOOD SUPPLY

DAM

Bats

Vespertilionidae

Bats are mammals that can fly. Their fore-feet are shaped in such a way as to form wings. Between the individual fingers and between the arms and the body and the hind legs are thin flaps of skin that form the wings.

Some bats are very large. "Flying foxes" may have a wingspan of 90 centi-metres (3 feet). Most bats, however, are smaller. The common pipistrelle, for example, has a wing span of only 19 centi-metres ($7\frac{3}{4}$ inches). It is commonly found around towns, villages and the countryside over Europe and most of Asia. Bats fly in the same way as birds. They flap their wings rapidly, about fifteen times a second.

During the day bats sleep in caves or hollow trees. They hang, head down, clinging to cracks or bumps with their short legs. Their wings are folded round them when they rest. In the evening the bats awaken and catch insects in the air.

Bats have poor eyesight, but they have echo location to guide them. While they are flying, they send out short calls, about five to ten squeaks each second. The calls are so high in pitch that we cannot hear them, but the bat can. When the sound waves hit something they bounce back like a ball, and the bat knows some obstacle is in front of it. In this way bats can catch even tiny insects. Two kinds of call can be uttered: normal squeaks which we can hear, and short-wave squeaks inaudible to human ears.

Bats use up a lot of energy in flying, so they have to eat a lot. A bat eats about one quarter of its own weight for every hour it spends hunting.

The male and female mate while they are hanging upside down. During the winter the sperm lives in the womb of the female bat. When spring comes, the egg is released and fertilized and starts growing. In early summer she bears her young while hanging upside down. The mother holds onto the ceiling, with her arms making a kind of pocket that the young will be caught in at birth time. The young open their eyes after one week. After two weeks they can hang from

Bats sleep upside down in caves

the ceiling by themselves. After three months they can take care of themselves.

When autumn comes the insectivorous bats settle down to hibernate. Throughout the winter they hang quietly upside down in their dark hideouts.

Some bats can live to be twenty years old, but most live only to be about five. Owls and cats catch them at night and, if they come out early, hawks hunt them, too.

The female bat hunts with her young clinging firmly to her underside

Food: insects

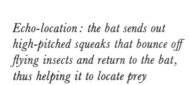

Echo-location: the bat sends out high-pitched squeaks that bounce off flying insects and return to the bat, thus helping it to locate prey

Deer

Cervidae

In their wild state the deer's keen eyes, ears and sense of smell usually discover us long before we discover them, and most of us do not have the opportunity of seeing them at close quarters. However, in winter, when hard pressed for food, some deer will venture closer to human habitation and raid country gardens.

There is great variation in the size of deer, from the tiny pudu of South America standing 34 centimetres (13½ inches) high at the shoulder, to the biggest of all deer,

the European elk, or moose, standing 182 centimetres (6 feet) high at the shoulder.

The outstanding feature of this group of animals is their antlers; some members have simple antlers, others have more developed antlers with wide branches and crowns. The musk-deer of Asia have no antlers at all.

The males, or bucks, as they are called, have antlers. These grow out and are shed each year. When the buck is two years old he grows his first set of antlers in the spring.

SPRING   SUMMER   AUTUMN

While they are growing, they are covered with soft skin, known as velvet. When autumn comes, the antlers have become strong and hard, and the buck brushes off the skin against trees and bushes. At first the antlers have only one point, but they develop year by year until the buck is in his prime and has twelve in all. The antlers are used for fighting other bucks. In the autumn, when the females, or does,

Two males fighting over a female

Food: leaves, buds, fruit, acorns

as they are called, are ready to mate, the bucks seek them out. Sometimes a buck has to fight other bucks to keep his doe. The bucks charge each other with their heads held low. The antlers clash together with a great noise. Usually no harm comes to the bucks. The weaker one runs away as soon as it sees it cannot win. Sometimes two bucks get their antlers interlocked and they cannot get free of each other. Then they will both die of starvation. When the mating season is over, the buck sheds its

old antlers, and new ones start to grow.

The young, or fawns, as they are called, are not born until spring. At that time the doe finds a dense and secret place in the woods. Here she gives birth to two fawns. They are of a pretty, reddish-brown colour, with rows of white spots along their backs. At first they are very helpless and just lie still while the doe goes out to eat or drink. But on the doe's nourishing milk they grow fast, and after a few months they are able to follow her. By then it is autumn, and it is almost time for the doe to mate again.

In winter the deer have a hard time finding things to eat. Because the snow covers the ground, they often have to eat bark from trees. In some places there is not enough food, and many deer die of hunger. But enough survive so that when spring comes, there are still plenty of deer.

Deer can reach an age of twenty years, but many die long before that.

A fawn's spots are camouflage. The fawn has no odour, and when it lies perfectly still, it is hard to detect

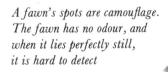

African Elephant

Loxodonta africana

The African elephant is the largest land animal in the world. It is 330 centimetres (11 feet) tall and weighs over 5000 kilograms (6 tons). Its trunk is 200 centimetres (7 feet) long. The trunk is very strong, and the elephant uses it as we use a hand. The elephant can reach up for food in high branches with its trunk; it can pick up a nut from the ground with the tip. When the elephant drinks, it sucks the water up its trunk. The water is then squirted into its mouth. When the elephant bathes, it throws water over its back.

The tusks of an elephant are in fact very large upper teeth. They can be up to 330 centimetres (11 feet) long and weigh up to 90 kilograms (200 pounds) apiece. The elephant uses them for digging roots out of the ground. Unfortunately for the elephant, its tusks are prized for their "ivory".

The African elephant has big ears. They can be 180 centimetres (6 feet) across. When it is very hot, the elephant stands in the shade waving its ears to keep itself cool.

Food: fruit, vegetation, roots

Elephants move about in herds. Most herds consist of mother elephants and their young. The herd rests early in the morning and during the hot hours of the afternoon. The elephants spend the remainder of the time eating and bathing. Even at night the elephants seek food. Each elephant eats 130 kilograms (300 pounds) of foliage a day and drinks 135 to 180 litres (30 to 40 gallons) of water. To find that amount of food it has to roam over a very large area. Every now and then the herd will be visited by a bull elephant. Most of the time, however, the bull stays by himself. When the female is ready to mate, she and the bull spend some time together and they mate. Soon the bull leaves her and she rejoins the herd. The female is pregnant for twenty-two months. Then she gives birth to the baby elephant. The baby stands one metre (3 feet) high and weighs 110 kilograms (250 pounds). It stays with its mother for about three years and is adult at about ten years old. The females give birth to baby elephants every four years.

Elephants may live to be about eighty years old. When they reach that age their teeth are worn down, and they die because they can no longer chew grass and leaves.

AFRICAN ELEPHANT

ASIAN ELEPHANT

AFRICAN ELEPHANT: TRUNK AND HIND FOOT (THREE NAILS)

ASIAN ELEPHANT: TRUNK AND HIND FOOT (FOUR NAILS)

Blue Whale

Balaenoptera musculus

Whales are mammals that have taken to the sea. Their shape has changed to resemble that of fishes. Their limbs resemble the fins of fish. But they still breathe with lungs and, therefore, they have to come to the surface quite often.

The largest whale, in fact the largest animal that has ever existed, is the blue whale. The blue whale weighs up to 15,000 kilograms (150 tons) and can be up to 30 metres (100 feet) long. It spends the summer in the cold waters of the Arctic and Antarctic oceans. Here the plankton and shrimps on which it lives are' very plentiful. The blue whale has an enormous mouth. It has no teeth, but from the upper jaw hang two rows of whalebone. Whalebone, or baleen, is really a large horny board, one edge of which is very ragged. The whalebone works like a sieve. When the whale takes a mouthful of

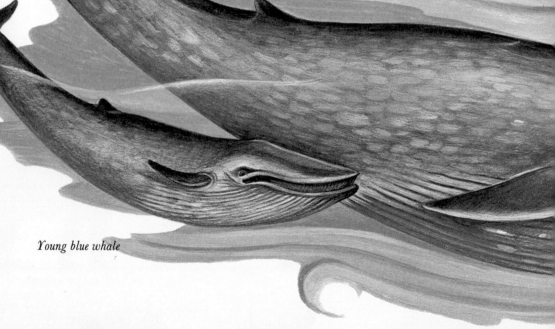

Young blue whale

Food: krill and large plankton

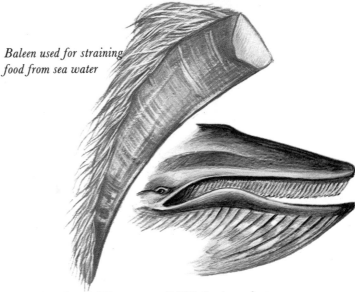

Baleen used for straining food from sea water

plankton, it presses the water out through the whalebone with its large tongue. Shrimps and other small crustaceans cannot escape and are swallowed. The blue whale eats more than 1000 kilograms of shrimps per day, and as much as 2000 kilograms have been found in its stomach. Two thousand kilograms of shrimps represent more than five million shrimps! Plankton and shrimps are found near the surface of the water, where the blue whale spends most of its time. But the blue whale can also dive very deep. It can reach a depth of 450 metres (1500 feet) and stay underwater for one hour. When it does come to the surface to breathe, it lets the air out of the breathing hole on top of its head with such force that the vapour jet will reach a height of 6 metres (20 feet) and more. Blue whales can swim at a speed of fifteen knots.

In winter blue whales migrate to warmer waters, either alone or in pairs. Blue whales mate out of the water. The male and the female swim towards each other, and when they meet, they shoot out of the water. For a few seconds their undersides are pressed together, and the mating takes place. The female blue whale is pregnant for almost eleven months. She then gives birth to a baby whale that is 7·5 metres (25 feet) long and weighs 2000 kilograms. For six months the baby lives on the mother's milk. The mother's milk glands produce 90 kilograms (200 pounds) of milk per day. After six months the whale has grown to be 15 metres (50 feet) long, and it can then fend for itself.

Skeleton of blue whale

REMAINS OF
PELVIC (HIP) BONE

Lion

Panthera leo

The lion lives in Africa. Many years ago it was also found in southern Europe and in parts of Asia. But like so many other wild animals, it has disappeared from many areas. This is because man has hunted it. The lion has no other enemies but man.

The lion is a very large cat. From the nose to the tip of the tail it is 3 metres (10 feet) long, and it weighs about 220 kilograms (500 pounds).

Lions live together in groups. They prefer open savanna where many antelopes and zebras graze in large herds. When lions hunt, they usually do so in groups. Some of the lions walk towards the herd of antelopes while one hides and sneaks up from another direction. When the antelopes are close enough, the lion jumps from its hiding place onto an antelope's neck, twists the head and breaks its victim's neck. Lions not only kill antelopes and zebras but have been known to kill rhinoceros and baby elephants.

A group of lions living together is called a "pride". Each pride usually consists of two females and their cubs. They kill an animal about every three days. When the

Food: game, such as antelope and zebras

females are ready to mate, a male lion will join them. The lioness does most of the hunting, even when she is pregnant, which is for three and a half months. When she gives birth to her four cubs, the male leaves her to find another female who will hunt for him.

Lion cubs are blind when they are born. Their eyes open when they are four days old. For three months they live on their mother's milk alone. When they are very young, they are spotted, almost like leopards. When they have been weaned, the mother starts taking the cubs along on hunting trips. At first they are very clumsy, but soon they learn to catch small animals. When they are two years old, they can hunt big game for themselves, and they may leave the pride to start families of their own.

The males have large territories, about 15 kilometres (10 miles) of savanna, which they defend against other males. Often the roaring of a lion is enough to scare others away, but sometimes the males fight and even kill one another. Lions may grow to be thirty years old.

Gorilla

Gorilla gorilla

The gorilla is the closest living relative of man. Yet it is very different. Most of its body is covered with hair. Although it can walk on its hind legs alone, it rarely does so. Like human beings it can oppose its thumbs to the fingers of its hand. Most important of all, the gorilla has a much smaller brain than a human brain. Gorillas cannot learn to talk. Although they can make about twenty different sounds of various meanings, they do not have a language as human beings do.

An adult male gorilla is about 180 centimetres (6 feet) tall when it stands up and weighs about 140 to 180 kilograms (300–400 pounds). Gorillas live in groups; the leader is an old male. Several females and their young make up the rest of the group. Sometimes other males join the group and live peacefully with the others. Most

groups consist of about fifteen gorillas. The gorillas spend most of the day seeking food. They live on plants and berries and are strictly vegetarian. They move about from place to place, and every night they build themselves nests or beds in which they sleep. On the ground the nests are made of leaves and a few branches. In trees they are made of branches that form a platform on which the gorilla can lie. In the morning gorillas wake up late. After breakfast the adults usually rest for a while, while the young play. Most of their time is spent on the ground.

Each group has a territory, about 24 square kilometres (15 square miles), where it seeks food. When two groups of gorillas meet at the border, they do not fight. The leaders stare at each other for a while. They might even threaten each other by

AFRICA

LOWLAND
GORILLAS

MOUNTAIN
GORILLAS

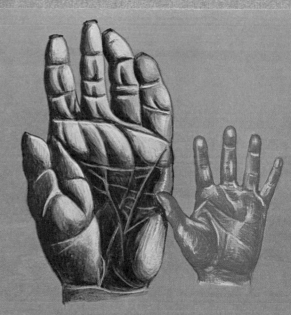

howling and banging their fists against their large chests. But after a while each group goes its own way. The real enemy of the gorilla is man. Although leopards and other large meat eaters prey upon the young they do not hunt the gorilla to near-extinction. Otherwise gorillas lead a very peaceful life.

Like human beings, the gorilla female has her period once a month, at which time the lining of the womb is expelled. If she has mated and becomes pregnant, her period stops. She is then pregnant for eight and a half months, when she delivers her baby gorilla. The baby gorilla weighs nearly 2 kilograms (4 pounds) at birth. It clings to its mother, who carries it about with her. When the baby gorilla is one month old, its eyes can focus. When it is eight months old, it is weaned and eats the same food as the other gorillas, but until it is two to two and a half years old, its mother has to carry it when the group travels. A male gorilla is fully grown when he is ten years old; a female takes six or seven years to reach maturity. Gorillas live to be about thirty years old. The female has a single young about every four years.

Food: vegetation, pineapple leaves, fruit, green bananas

Comparison of gorilla's hand and human hand

Human Being

Homo sapiens

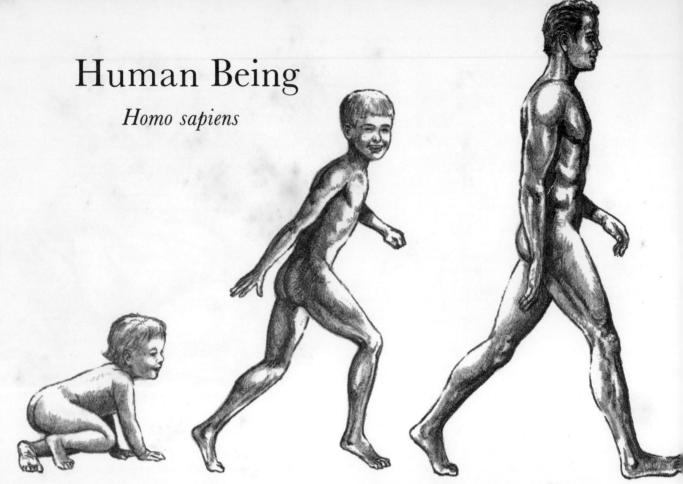

The human being, or man, is an animal. Our closest relatives in the animal kingdom are the apes, gorillas, chimpanzees, gibbons, and orang-utans. With them and other monkeys we belong to the group called primates.

Although man in many ways resembles other mammals, he is also different in a number of ways. Let us look at these differences.

Man walks upright on two legs. Most mammals walk on four legs. By walking on two legs, the arms and hands are free to do many other things. Our hands are very different from the hands (or forefeet) of most other mammals. Monkeys and apes are mammals with hands and most of them, but not all, can move their thumbs against the other fingers to pick up objects and hold them. With his hands man has made all the machines he needs, the clothes he wears, and many other things.

The brain of man has developed further than that of any other animal. The most important part is that which makes it possible for us to learn and understand a language. No other animal can learn so many words, and no other animal has the ability to connect different words into sentences.

Other animals can give information to one another with their voices. For instance, a bird tells other birds where its territory is by singing, or it might warn other birds of danger by its alarm call. But even though a parrot can learn to say certain words or even sentences, it will never be able to understand the meaning of the word, or put words together into sentences. Men can give information by writing and reading as well as by speech.

So even though we resemble other animals in many ways, we are still very different.

Man first lived in areas where it was warm and he did not need clothes. But as he moved to other parts of the world, his naked skin could no longer protect him from the cold. So he covered himself with

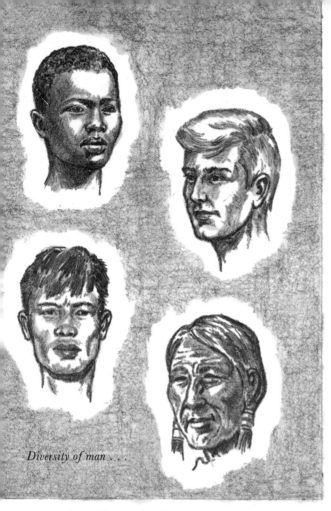

Diversity of man . . .

Cows eat plants and would not eat meat; cows are herbivorous (*herbi* meaning plants). Lions eat meat and would not eat plants; lions are carnivorous (*carni* meaning meat). But man eats both meat and plants and many other things besides.

Food: man is omnivorous

the skins of other animals. Later he learned to weave.

Man is omnivorous. This means he can eat (*vorus*) eveything (*omni*). Of course, man does not eat everything. We do not eat stones, nails, earth, and so on, but we do have a varied diet, unlike most other animals, who have a specialized diet.

The first human beings lived on insects, seeds, fruits, and other things they could find easily. They also hunted small animals. When they learned to make axes and spears, they hunted large animals.

. . . and the way he lives

POLAR

TROPICAL

TEMPERATE

93

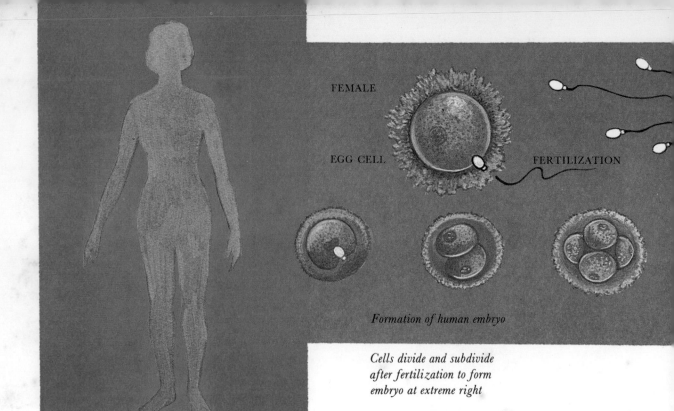

FEMALE

EGG CELL   FERTILIZATION

Formation of human embryo

Cells divide and subdivide
after fertilization to form
embryo at extreme right

Later they learned to sow seeds and to harvest. They also started to domesticate various animals, such as cows, horses, pigs, sheep, and chickens. In this way they did not have to travel to find their food—they became farmers. When farming became so efficient that each farmer could produce more food than he himself could eat, he bartered his extra for goods. This meant that blacksmiths, carpenters, and many other craftsmen, could trade their products and skills for food. Fishermen could trade their fish for grain and other necessary items. Over many, many, years farming became more and more efficient, and today only a few people are needed to produce all the food the millions of people living today need.

When a human baby is born, it is very helpless. At first it lives on its mother's milk alone, but it can soon start eating strained food. As the baby grows, it first learns to follow things with its eyes. It is about six weeks old when this happens. When it is eight months old, it can sit, and by one year it can start walking. Most

4 WEEKS (6 mm)   6 WEEKS (12 mm)   8 WEEKS (25 mm)

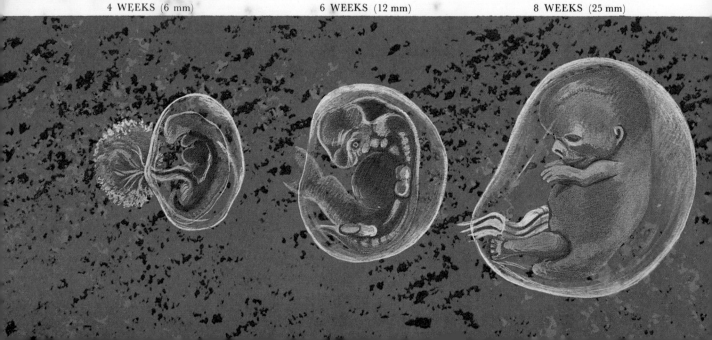

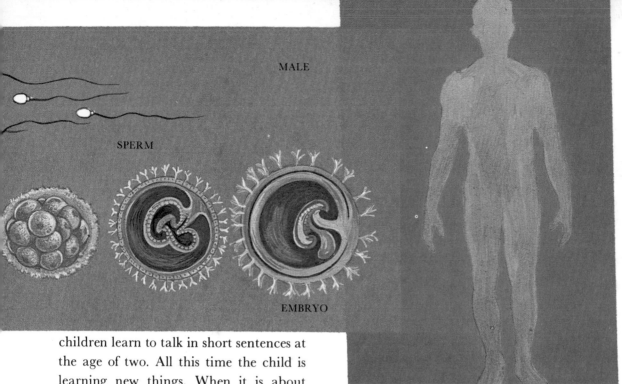

MALE

SPERM

EMBRYO

children learn to talk in short sentences at the age of two. All this time the child is learning new things. When it is about eleven to thirteen years old, it has reached sexual maturity, but it does not stop growing until it has reached seventeen to nineteen years of age. When girls reach sexual maturity, they start menstruating. Each month the womb expels its lining through the vagina, and a new lining grows. Between two menstruations an egg is released into the womb. If the egg is fertilized by a sperm cell, which enters through the vagina, it attaches itself to the lining of the womb, which is then not expelled. Instead, the egg grows. It receives its food through the lining of the womb. After nine months the egg has grown into a baby,

which is born through the vagina. The sperm comes from the testes, the man's sex glands. When the penis is inserted into the vagina of the woman, the sperm is released and travels into the womb where the egg is formed.

Most people marry and have children when they are in their twenties. At this time most have learned a trade by which they can earn enough money to support a family.

Human beings can live to be more than one hundred years of age, but most people die before they are seventy years old.

3 MONTHS (57 mm)   4 MONTHS (203 mm)   9 MONTHS, BIRTH POSITION (485–530 mm)

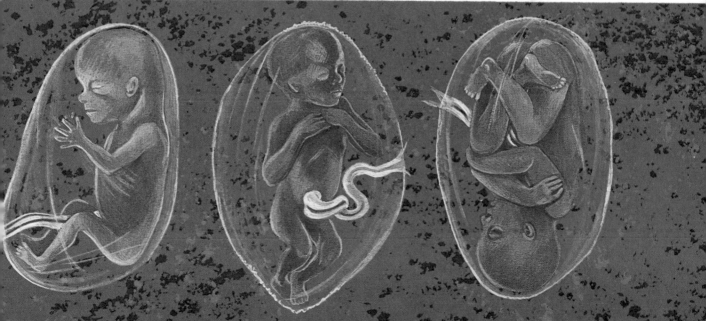